Waddington on Salmon Fishing

Waddington on Salmon

FISHING

RICHARD WADDINGTON

The Crowood Press

First published in 1991 by
The Crowood Press Ltd
Gipsy Lane, Swindon
Wiltshire SN2 6DQ

British Library Cataloguing in Publication Data

Waddington, Richard
Waddington on salmon fishing
1. Salmon. Angling
I. Title
799.1755

ISBN 1 85223 496 2

Acknowledgements
The author is grateful to the following for use of black
and white photographs. Pages 23 and 147 J. Allan Cash;
page 53 Conrad Voss Bach; pages 62, 65 and 100 Donald
B. MacCulloch; page 73 William B. Currie; pages 99 and
110 G. L. Carlisle; pages 70, 90 and 105 L. S. Paterson;
page 82 Wildlife Services; page 89 Fox Photos Ltd; and
pages 118 and 149 The Norwegian Tourist Board.
The author is also grateful to the following for the use
of colour photographs. Plates 14, 19, 20, 21 and 22 A. D.
Gowans; plates 4, 15 and 17 Roy Shaw; plates 6, 8 and 11
The Malcolm Innes Gallery; plate 9 Christie's Colour
Library; plate 10 The Tate Gallery; plate 13 Dave Pike;
plate 5 The Highlands and Islands Development Board;
and plates 1, 3, 18, 23 and 24 Salar Properties (UK) Ltd.

Printed and bound in Great Britain by
BPCC Hazell Books
Aylesbury, Bucks, England
Member of BPCC Ltd.

Contents

Foreword

Sixty-eight years ago Richard Waddington caught his first salmon – a 7-pounder from the Aberdeenshire Dee. Since that time many hundreds of salmon have fallen prey to this ace fisher – most, I imagine, victims of his own invention, the deadly Waddington articulated fly.

I first met Richard Waddington some thirty years ago, when, as a youthful sporting journalist I used to spend my weekends ghillying on the Herefordshire Wye, at Glasbury. The local hotel had an indifferent piece of water available to residents which boasted the most abominable fishing boat imaginable. It was a punt, of the type quite at home on a bream-fisher's Cheshire mere, but virtually useless on a river swollen by spring rain.

We set sail in the horrid craft, nudging out beyond the overhanging trees. The current struck the broad bow and my best efforts to hold the boat proved unequal to the task. I dropped the anchor and Richard Waddington showed me how to hold the boat in a fishable position. He then proceeded to fish with great skill. Much as I should like to be able to tell you that we caught a number of fish that day, truth must out. Conditions were atrocious, the river rising into red flood, and no sport was forthcoming.

While he fished, Richard Waddington talked about fish and fishing. It became obvious to me that here was a thinking angler – a man whose knowledge of salmon fishing was tremendous; one who took nothing for granted but who held fascinating theories based on his vast experience.

Despite the lack of fish, that day taught me a great deal, and I have since held Richard Waddington in great esteem. His latest book is controversial and thought-provoking which, as there are no hard-and-fast rules in salmon fishing, is just what a salmon-fishing book should be.

Sandy Leventon
Trout and Salmon magazine

The Salmon's Story – the Early Months

Among field sports salmon fishing occupies a unique place. The sportsman who foxhunts, who shoots with shotgun or rifle, engages himself in hunting down an animal and killing it. The angler, by contrast, hopes to run across a hungry fish which can be tempted to join in a sporting contest by accepting the offer of a tempting morsel. Among anglers the salmon fisher stands alone. His prize, unlike other fish he might encounter, has not only lost all its feeding teeth, may not yet have started to replace them and has a digestive system which has atrophied and is non-functional. The salmon is replete with stored fat and energy in body tissue and is well prepared for a fast which will last for many months. Indeed when looked at rationally it would seem absurd that anyone, knowing these facts, would set out to fish for salmon by casting something into the water and expecting a fish to remove itself from its comfortable lie and attempt to eat it. Nevertheless this is exactly what the salmon angler does. And I regret to say that most of them do it without giving any thought to the reasons for fishing in the manner they have chosen. Salmon fishing is more than a sport. Salmon fishing is an art and it is an art which requires thought and study as well as practice.

The first thing that the serious fisherman must study is the fish itself. The life story of the salmon is one of the most incredible romances in nature. Had this story been invented no-one would have believed it. It is a story which at every stage seems almost impossible. Yet unbelievable though it may be, this is a truth which really is stranger than fiction.

It starts in the fall of the year. By the end of October the salmon have reached the spawning beds and with the first frosts will start to lay their eggs and fertilize them. Deposited in 'redds' dug out of the coarsest gravel and rock, these eggs, the next generation of salmon, are now abandoned by their parents who leave the upper reaches of the river and make their way back to the sea.

The observer's first reaction must be that this is a strange time of year for any creature to lay its eggs and then to desert them. The coldest part of the winter is still to come. Moreover the salmon chooses the cold uplands rather than the milder lowlands and is careful to build the redd in a strong stream rather than in the deeper and calmer areas of a pool. Nature herself, as ever, provides the explanation. The salmon egg takes anything from forty to seventy days to hatch. The incubation time depends upon the water temperature – the lower the temperature the longer the time. Furthermore, as Frank Buckland, the 'father' of artificial hatching noted, the best results arrive when the eggs take a long time to hatch. 'Keep your temperatures low' he advised his workforce. There is a perfectly good scientific reason for this. Incubating eggs need oxygen and also have to dispose of carbon dioxide (CO_2), both of which must pass through the membrane which encloses the egg. The oxygen is dissolved in the river water from the air, and it is in the coldest waters where the highest density of the most easily available oxygen is to be found. Likewise the colder the water the more CO_2 it can dissolve and

The Boat pool at Crathie on the River Dee, with Balmoral Castle in the distance.

hold in solution. Also cold upland streams do not have vegetation which, by photosynthesis, gives off CO_2 at night and often saturate the water in solution. When this occurs the egg cannot eliminate the CO_2 which is one of the waste products of the growing embryo. It must perish. It must be remembered also that the speed at which the embryo develops is dependent upon the temperature. The warmer the water, the quicker the development and consequently, the greater the demand for oxygen and for the elimination of CO_2 at any and every moment. At the same time, because it is warmer, the water holds less oxygen in solution and can dissolve less CO_2.

It is clear that the eggs need cold, well-oxygenated water and hatch better over longer periods of time. That the salmon times its spawning to conform with these requirements seems remarkable. It is at hatching that the beauty of this fish's timing is revealed.

The hatched alevin is in fact in no sense fully hatched. The tiny fish has broken out of the membrane which enclosed the growing embryo, but has left it still attached to the remaining contents of the egg. This will provide it with sustenance, entirely at first, in part later, for about six weeks. Once the egg's contents have been absorbed the young fish is reliant on food being carried to it by the stream. It is still sheltering behind stones in the redd and will probably make these its home for several months. If the winter has been comparatively warm after a frosty October with the egg being fertilized on, say, 1 November, it will hatch in about forty days ... about 10 December, and the alevin will have absorbed its yolk sac six weeks later ... about mid-January. It now needs food, but where is it to find it? It is still midwinter and the river can provide nothing until the inflorescence of spring brings the diatom growth. So this early-spawned, early-hatched fish must die. An egg laid a month later in a warm winter will have only a slightly better chance of producing a fish which can survive. It will now be almost March before the alevin becomes totally dependent on food produced by the river. This is still too early. It will be seen that with the exception of very late, perhaps late-December/January spawning, the young fish hatched after a mild winter will not generally survive.

In cold, hard winters, by contrast, everything favours the survival of the young parr. Even the early spawned alevins will not be free of the yolk sac until late February/early March; the later spawnings will produce parr ready to feed at the height of the spring inflorescence and will thus be well established by the time the main insect hatches of early summer take place.

Whether it is by Darwinian natural selection, as some scientists affirm, or by the direct intervention of the Almighty, the sequence of events which leads to the successful hatching of a young salmon and its establishment safely in the redd seem quite miraculous. First, the salmon do not start to

9

The Greymare at Cairnton on the River Dee.

spawn until the water temperature has dropped so much that in a normal winter the egg is able to survive. It cannot live if, in a too-warm river, the embryo develops so quickly that it cannot either obtain sufficient oxygen or is poisoned by the by-products of embolism. Consequently the season for spawning is delayed until the best chance is offered of the eggs developing as slowly as possible and hatching as near to the spring inflorescences as possible. As an insurance policy, the fact that the spawning season may last as long as seven or eight weeks renders it virtually certain that no climatic disaster can destroy all of any one generation. In warm winters all the early-spawned eggs may perish, and all the early-hatched alevins may die. However, the late and very late spawners will have produced eggs which hatch successfully into alevins which can survive.

I have often heard riparian owners and river keepers complain that the early formed redds are being dug up by the late-spawning fish. They should not complain but should welcome this. If anything destroys the offspring of the early fish there will be an ample stock of parr deriving from the late spawners. If the weather in spring is unusually cold the springing to life of the diatoms and insects may be delayed. This, too, may spell disaster to the early spawned and hatched alevins. Again it is the offspring of the late spawners which come to the rescue. Our egg which first, after fertilization turned into an 'eyed ova', then into an alevin carrying a yolk sac and finally into a perfect little fish (the parr), is now a trout-like creature. Banded and trout-coloured it will feed on whatever the river brings to it in the way of insect life for the next year, perhaps two, or three – even four or five in some of the very cold rivers of the north. The next stage of its life cannot be achieved until it has grown to at least four inches in length. The rate of growth will depend upon the food supply. Where there is plenty it grows quickly. In the year in which it achieves a length of four inches plus during the month of May, it starts the change into the next stage of its life cycle.

Journey to the Sea

We have left our baby salmon, now entirely dependent upon what the river brings it for food, sheltering still between the stones of the redd in which it hatched out. It will stay here for several weeks, even months, and will gradually learn to make sorties into the river. At first it is entirely dependent on the stream washing items of food into the crevice in which it is sheltering. But as it grows it becomes bolder and begins searching in the deeper water and the pools. Before winter comes the little parr no longer seeks the shelter of the redd but is now shoaling up with others of its own generation in the open river.

The salmon is not herbivorous. It is an insectivore and a carnivore. From the moment it has consumed the contents of the yolk sac it seeks protein food deriving from larvae, insects, worms and grubs or from dead and decaying animal matter. As it grows, like all the *Salmo* genus, it becomes a hunter of larger living insects and of small fish, molluscs and crustaceans. The salmon parr in its river surroundings behaves almost identically like a trout of the same age. It looks very like a trout, it hunts the same things and, to the annoyance of trout fishermen, is caught on the same flies which trout take. It is during this period of its life that two things become imprinted upon its tiny brain. First, that hunting for food and growing as big and as fast as possible is its No 1 priority and second is the memory of the redd where it originated and the return route it must travel when it is its turn to create another generation of salmon.

The only reason that salmon, essentially freshwater fish, ever went to sea was because they found that they grew bigger and more quickly on the easily obtained abundance of food in the sea. When our fish returns to the river after its sojourn in the sea there is imprinted on its mind the memory of how, in its parr days, it caught hatching flies, and took the larvae of various water insects, snails and shrimps. It was born a hunter, grew up a hunter and the search for food was, until it returned to the river of its birth, the only interest in its life. So strongly was this passion for hunting for food imprinted in the salmon that the fish, as a species, had to learn to travel thousands of miles to satisfy it. It is perhaps little to be wondered at that, even though unable to digest food when returning to freshwater, the salmon at times remembers that it is primarily a hunter?

It is on this memory that the angler relies when he casts his fly and hopes that a salmon will take it. Without this memory of a lifetime of hunting and feeding the fasting fish could never be tempted into taking any fly or bait.

The young salmon has many enemies. First and foremost must be the changing moods of the river itself. Ice formed in heavy frosts while the alevins and parr are still in the redds can, when a sudden thaw comes, destroy most of the redds as it is carried downstream. All the hatched alevins, all the unhatched eggs and most of the young parr will be destroyed by great blocks of ice so powerful in a swollen stream that the course of the river itself is often carved out anew. Big spates, too, spell danger. The little fish, a powerful swimmer, is not in danger of being carried away, but in seeking shelter is liable, when the water falls, to find itself stranded in a shallow pool which is not part of the river. The parr faces dangers too in periods of very low water. The excessive use of chemical weed and pest killers as well as manures and, far too often, the discharge of slurry and other farm waste into the river, which is the fish's environment, can become so toxic as to destroy all life. There are many examples of rivers where, though salmon had once been able to enter, to survive as mature fish and to breed successfully in the headwaters, no young fish have recently been able to survive in the polluted river. The salmon runs have ended.

It is perhaps quite surprising that only a very small proportion of the eggs that the salmon lays in the redd (about 700 for every pound of her weight) do not find safe and successful lodges among the stones. A small number are washed down the stream and are scavenged by waiting trout. More are dislodged when the early redds are dug up by late spawners when, again, some eggs are eaten by trout. On the whole, however, few river fish pick up food which is lying on the bottom and the salmon's egg is appreciably heavier than fresh water. Nevertheless the chance of any alevin hatching from such eggs must be very remote indeed.

In the cool and rather acid waters of our northern rivers the food supply (mainly insect larvae and nymphs) will not be as readily available as in the warmer waters with higher Ph value of more southern streams. In the former it may take appreciably longer for the parr to achieve the size required for it to become a smolt. In the cold Icelandic and Norwegian rivers, for instance, many parr require five years growing in the river before they achieve sufficient size to make the journey to the sea. By contrast, in such southern streams as the Hampshire Avon and the French and Spanish Atlantic-flowing rivers, parr which achieve smolt stage after only one year are common. The rate of growth of the young fish depends, then, on how easily food is found. As soon as it achieves a length of four inches plus in the month of May, it undergoes the first of the four physical and physiological changes which it will suffer during the remainder of its life. The fifth will almost certainly cause its death.

The little fish now prepares for a long journey into completely unknown and strange surroundings and for a life in an atmosphere which is totally different from that in which it has so far lived. It must prepare to move from fresh water into salt water. Its first move is to don a special migratory dress. Within a few days its banded trout-like coloration has disappeared under the silver coat of guanin which it will wear over its banded dress throughout its life at sea. The little parr has now become a smolt, a miniature of the sea going salmon. If it fed vigorously as a parr, now as a smolt, it becomes voracious. Shoaling up with others who are migrating they become what looks to the fisherman like a myriad of jewels flashing in the afternoon sunshine as they descend through the pool. Every fisherman will recognize the beginning of the smolt migration. It is often impossible to cast even quite large flies into the pool without one of these little creatures taking it.

Feeding its way to the sea, the young salmon now hits the brackish water where a further change occurs. So far it has survived in the face of many dangers from a variety of enemies. Possibly the most dangerous have been trout, even quite small trout, which readily eat salmon parr. Large cannibal trout takes these as well as the young of their own species and migrating smolts of both salmon and sea trout. Obviously in rivers and lakes where there are pike, these too account for large numbers of parr and smolts. Of animal predators probably only the mink would concern himself with such small prey, but there are a number of birds ranging from the dipper, which is said to eat salmon eggs, to kingfishers and herons which certainly eat small fish in great quantities. Deadly enemies, too, are goosanders, mergansers and the odd cormorant whose only food from the river is small fish.

Arriving in the brackish water of the sea pool the smolt faces new hazards. Until it reaches the deeper waters of the open ocean the migrating smolt must run the gauntlet of a host of enemies. Virtually every larger fish in the coastal waters of the sea will kill and eat smolts making their way out of the river. Not only must they avoid this danger, but the smolts, at the same time, have to undergo a profound change in their physical make up.

A typical salmon river.

They are now moving from fresh to salt water. First, they 'weigh less' in salt water – they are more buoyant. Secondly, the refractive index of salt water differs from that of fresh and also from the aqueous humours in the fish's eye. Things look different and distances are more difficult to gauge. But outweighing all these problems is the danger it faces from literally drying out. Put simply, the fish's body cells contain a saline solution which is less salty than sea water. The cells are surrounded by a permeable membrane which allows water to pass through it from a less salty solution, the cell contents, into a saltier solution, sea water. This exchange is activated by osmotic pressure. Except for one area of its body the fish prevents its cells from drying out by covering them with its skin which is impermeable. The one vulnerable area is the gills. Through them the fish is constantly losing water from its body into the sea. To replace this it must literally drink sea water, filter the salt from it via its kidney, and thus replace the lost liquid. It will be seen that if the fish suffers any injury which causes tears or losses of its impermeable skin the problem of drying out is aggravated. Severe injuries, such as are sometimes suffered in escaping from nets, will inevitably be fatal.

The journey to its pelagic feeding grounds is accomplished as far as is known with despatch and as little delay as possible. On the way it will feed on a whole variety of crustacea, fish, copepods, molluscs, cephalopods and octopods which abound where the margins of that greatest of all rivers, the Gulf Stream, mingle with the cold waters of the Arctic. It will hunt and feed and grow throughout the coming months. Most of the salmon born in British rivers together with those of Norway and Iceland will feed for the greater part of their sea lives off the coast of Greenland. Salmon originating in the Baltic area tend not to leave that sea and, curiously, have been fished for, as immature feeding fish, with set lines off the Island of Bornholm for many centuries.

In its ocean feeding grounds the Atlantic salmon faces one enemy of special significance. Too fast a swimmer to be caught easily by other predatory fish, growing too large to be taken by fishing birds, the salmon is a favourite and comparatively easily caught prey of seals of every sort. No one has yet estimated what proportion of immature and feeding salmon are taken every year by seals. Surprisingly large numbers escape from these mammals bearing often hideous injuries from which they have managed to survive. The ominous warning signs which the virtual cessation of sealing as an industry gives to those who have the well-being of the salmon stocks in mind are obvious. A seal is said to eat its own weight of fish within a week. Where there are salmon these will form a proportion of this food, and if the seals are allowed to multiply unchecked the effect upon the salmon stocks

The Potarch Bridge pool on the River Dee – one of the great holding pools which feeds the middle and upper beats.

must inevitably spell disaster. However, it would seem that nature herself takes a hand. If man no longer checks the unnatural growth in the seal population by hunting them, then, as we have seen in 1988, disaster, in the shape of a deadly disease, can strike and virtually wipe out all the seals in a very large area of sea and coast.

Except for the clear priority of staying alive, the salmon's main and practically only interest lies in catching food and growing as fast as possible. The main foods which are most abundant and easily available in the cool waters of the Denmark Strait, where most of the salmon from both sides of the Atlantic feed, are fish and crustaceans. Capelin (sardine-sized fish) – the young of herring and sprats, both highly nutritious and full of fat, and small cod, ling and other young of the *Gadus* genus undoubtedly form a greater part of the staple diet of the feeding salmon during the cooler part of the year.

Besides these fish the salmon certainly feed for part of the year on shrimps and prawns which abound where the cold and warm waters meet as the Gulf Stream bends eastwards past Greenland and Iceland. It might be significant that a few of these crustaceans are red in colour! Many believe that the pinkness of the salmon's flesh is derived from a diet of crustaceans. It is certainly true, as everyone who has reared trout in stew ponds will know, that if fed with freshwater shrimps the flesh of trout becomes quite pink. Significant too is the fact that also abundant in these waters are a great variety of squid and octopus. It may well be that the awful effect that a spinning prawn fished down a pool can sometimes have in panicking numbers of salmon into leaving could be attributed to the fact that most of the cephalopods use the emission of a noxious 'ink' as a defensive mechanism. No doubt the salmon has good reason to remember this. Abundant, too, in these waters are a great variety of marine worms and invertebrates which the fish may well remember as special tit-bits.

The only other possible regular item of nourishment taken by the fish is one that has been suggested many times, but never proved – the Atlantic eel. The eel travels the length of the Gulf Stream to reach its breeding ground in the Sargasso sea. It lays its eggs and dies. The eggs hatch out in the Gulf of Mexico and the tiny leaf-like leptocephali set out on a momentous journey to the river from which their parents emanated. They travel slowly, feeding probably on diatoms and minute insects in the eddies of the edge of the mighty river. It takes the eel leptocephalus no less than three years to make the journey during which time it grows from a transparent leaf of less than a fingernail in size into a semi-transparent leaf of around two inches. It is perhaps worth noting that at its smallest the leptocephalus is living in the warmest water. As it grows so does it travel into cooler currents. Many have correlated this fact with the necessity of using smaller and smaller flies as the river falls and the temperature rises. We shall look at this again later. But for one fact the attractive proposal that the returning salmon follows the same path as the young eels and feeds on them on its way might carry conviction. The fact is that on starting its return journey the fish ceases to feed, loses its feeding teeth and suffers from a digestive system which atrophies. Though the fish may retain a partial instinct and desire to hunt, it is not hungry and it cannot eat.

We have looked in some detail at the salmon, its start in life, its enemies, its feeding habits and its migration into a strange atmosphere of which it has no knowledge and in which it will journey thousands of miles over a route of which it can know nothing. We can see many birds on migration being led by parent birds who themselves have been led by their parents on the same journey. We can understand that the leaders, in these cases, have travelled the way before and have the route imprinted on their memories. But young salmon entering the sea at a time when all fish of previous generations are either in the river or are approaching it, must not only know their ultimate destination, but also the route to it and the way back. The miracle of the

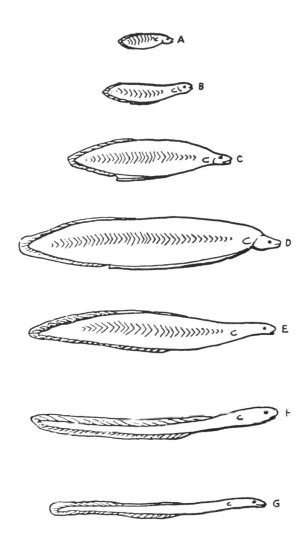

Growth of the elver (actual size)

migrating salmon is that it not only makes this remarkable journey, but that it can find its way back to the very spawning bed in which the egg from which it sprang was deposited. If this ability to find the way to a specific feeding ground must be ascribed to instinct (a most unsatisfactory way of explaining something we do not understand), then the return over the same course can at least be explained by memory. And if the fish's memory of a journey which it made some eighteen months previously is so good that it can retrace its steps in a totally unmarked route, then I do not think that the fish's memory of something which has occupied its whole life for several years can surprise us if it sometimes allows it to remember that it is primarily a hunting creature.

The Salmon Runs

It is said that there is no one day in the year when no salmon attempt to run the Spey. Of course the major migrations of spring and perhaps of July will be noted as the main means of stocking the river. Even these, though, are extended over several weeks. Before, in between, and after them there is always a trickle of fish which will run the river unless the water is so low that they are unable to enter.

There is, however, no corresponding trickle of smolts leaving. All descend within the space of two or three weeks. Some, the lucky feeders, will be but two years old. Others will be a year, possibly even two years older. The question is why, if they all leave the river at almost the same time, do they not all return at least in the same month? I do not think that any answer can be given that is other than a guess. Perhaps when those who can recall the days of the famous run of 'Blue Cocks' in September and October in the Spey will remember that these beautiful fresh fish, which were additional to and easily distinguishable from the normal autumn runs, were hardly ever seen above Delfur and never as far up as Craigellachie. Practically all of them stayed in the six miles of the Gordon Castle water. They will also recall that the Duke of Richmond and Gordon reared many thousands of parr to the smolt stage in hatcheries and stew ponds. These were situated at Gordon Castle itself and were within a few miles of the mouth of the river. It was from these that the smolts were released into the Spey. The average rod catch in the Duke's water, Orton and Gordon Castle, between 26 August and 15 October each year was over 600 fish! When the hatchery closed down the Blue Cocks started to disappear. Today none are left.

The disappearance of this famous run of autumn Spey fish, which corresponded with the closing down of the Gordon Castle hatchery, gave strong support to the obvious and generally correct belief that the date of entry of any salmon into the river depended to a great extent upon the distance that the fish had to travel to reach its predetermined spawning area. This spawning area, indeed the very site of the redds, would be that where the fish itself was born. The salmon which derived from a redd in the headwaters of a big river would return very early in the winter – so early, even, that as a 'springer' it would be entering with the late fish of the previous season's autumn run. The late runs of autumn salmon would, by contrast, be destined for spawning in the lower reaches of the river and its tributary streams.

The Spey Blue Cocks went no farther than Gordon Castle because the hatcheries and stew ponds where they were reared were no further up river than this. They arrived full of spawn, sexually very mature and with a full set of breeding (or should it be 'fighting') teeth. They spawned almost entirely in the shallows between the pools of the main river. With the later runs of these true autumn fish came also the earliest runs of the following season's spring fish, uncoloured, sexually immature, toothless and destined to spawn some eleven or twelve months later in the headwaters of the river. Today, when the closing dates for rod fishing in many rivers have been changed from the end of October to varying dates in September, few of these very early springers are caught in the autumn in any of the north-cast rivers. When eventually caught in the spring of the following season they can be recognised as being salmon which have been in the river for several months, genuine springers which have entered with the later autumn runs of the previous season.

If further support is needed for the proposal that the date of entry of a salmon is dependent to a great extent upon the distance which it has to travel to its breeding place is needed, then we have only to look at some of the many other examples which demonstrate this clearly. If, for instance, we look at the river system which comprises the Ness, Loch Ness, the Moriston, the Oich and the Garry we see that virtually no early spring fish are caught in the River Ness. All the early winter and spring fish run straight through the River Ness, into the loch and through it into the Garry river, via the Oich and the loch of that name. Others entering the River Ness make straight for the Moriston. A few grilse and summer salmon are caught in the Ness, but it is not until the rains of the month of August that the main salmon runs arrive in the river – those which stay in the river and which do not make straight for Loch Ness and its feeding streams. Other good examples are the river Orchy and the Awe. The earliest fish entering the Awe all make straight for the Orchy which is, of course, really the Upper Awe.

Most other rivers of the north-east of Scotland also had huge runs of autumn fish which entered each year after all netting, both river and sea,

Fly-fishing on the River Awe.

ceased by law (26 August). The Aberdeenshire Dee had excellent autumn fishing in the lower beats such as Banchory House and Ardoe through which the spring fish ran straight, never stopping. The River Don used to have an autumn run of large salmon which equalled, if it did not exceed, that of the Tay. In pre-war days it was not uncommon for over twenty fish to be taken by a single rod on both 'Snuffy' and 'Benjie' on the lower Grandhome stretch of this river in early October. The Don autumn run produced big fish almost as far upstream as Alford and I can remember a day when fifteen fish were taken from the pools in the well-named 'Paradise' beat of Monymusk in the middle stretches of this river.

There was no hatchery on the lower Don. This fact in no way reduced the enormous numbers of fish which comprised the autumn run, which lacked only the quality which the addition of the Blue Cocks would have given. But the fact that there were cruives effectively prevented salmon running the river during the netting season (11 February to 26 August) except during the statutory open time, which was twenty-four hours on a Sunday. Since, however, excuses were nearly always found . . . spates or drift wood etc . . .

The Rampot on the Paradise beat of Monymusk. A good holding pool on the well-named beat of the River Don.

to prevent the opening of the cruives, they often remained for weeks on end a total barrier to running fish. Since many pools up as far as Inverurie were netted from time to time any salmon which managed to get over the cruives in high water or on a Sunday was almost certainly caught. On 26 August all netting stopped and the cruives finally opened.

Within a few days, certainly with the first end of summer rains, the autumn run of salmon would begin. These fish, already reddening and heavy with spawn would fill the pools of the lower river. Here they provided some of the most sought-after fishing of the season. Had anyone suggested then that within a few years the autumn run, not only in the Don and the Dee but in most of the north-east rivers, would have disappeared, they would have been considered almost insane. Yet this has happened. With the exception of the Tay and to a certain extent the Tweed, both of which are in a sense special cases, the autumn runs which were such a feature of the great spring fishing rivers of the north have disappeared. Why? You may well ask.

When one of these rivers is looked at as an ecological whole an answer, if not *the* answer, to this question becomes clear. The river provides not only

Benjie pool on the lower Don. The photograph shows scum and pollution caused by paper mill effluent which, curiously, seems to have little effect on the fish.

the atmosphere which the salmon breathes, the medium in which it moves and travels, but also the food which supports its offspring from birth through the growing years until it reaches the sea. A pure and unadulterated river can supply a given amount of food only. If this same river is now literally poisoned to a greater or a lesser degree by, say toxic agricultural chemicals, then though its toxicity may not be sufficient to kill the fish, its capacity to produce food is reduced, and the number of young salmon which it can support is likewise reduced.

This reduction in ability to support the growth of alevins and parr is by no means the same throughout the length of the river. The upper river, for instance, will be largely free of contamination by weeds and pest-killing chemicals from intensively farmed land while the middle and lower river may be so toxic that all young fish life is unable to survive. Most rivers, too, have villages, towns and even large cities discharging industrial waste and sewage more or less directly into them. Again the upland headwaters are little affected by this. The middle and lower reaches though, may be so toxic and lacking in oxygen as to prevent any alevins surviving or even any eggs hatching.

The consequence of this variation in ability to allow the hatching of eggs and in supporting the growth of very young fish in different parts of the river leads eventually to a situation where only the parr deriving from spawning beds in the upper river survive to become smolts. And since, in principle, the date of entry into the river depends to a large extent upon the distance that the fish has to travel to reach its proper spawning bed, that where it hatched out, we can see that if there are no salmon spawning in the lower reaches, then there will be no late run of fish which should spawn there.

Furthermore, if we allow that one or two fish manage to spawn successfully in the lower reaches and that some of the alevins hatch out, what, we may ask is their chance of survival? The answer is virtually none! Firstly, in a polluted river there is little food of any sort, and most of this is taken by trout and any other mature fish. Secondly, when the smolt migration from the upper reaches is in full swing these voracious little salmon will quickly finish off any protein food which can be found. And this will be at a time when the alevins will have just consumed their yolk sacs and must find food for themselves.

The picture becomes clear. These great autumn runs have disappeared because, in what may be called 'the old days', the spring run of salmon was practically netted out both in the sea and in the river itself. Consequently the middle and upper river was, in general terms, stocked only by fish which entered before 11 February. These fish, very early runners, spawned early

26

for the most part in beds which were not disturbed by much later spawning summer fish. These, after the nets had taken their toll, were too few to matter. The great autumn run, spawning in the shallows of a still unpolluted lower river, were able to reproduce themselves with a generation of young fish that could find ample food for which there was little competition in its then cleaner waters.

With the removal of most of the nets in the rivers themselves and with the weekend 'open' time often doubled, the spring and summer runs, hitherto practically netted out, were allowed to increase to such an extent that not only did rod fishing in the middle and upper reaches become the most valuable for sport, but an additional weight of spawners was added to the redd areas of all the upper rivers. Until the salmon feeding grounds were discovered off Greenland, and until monofil nylon nets made catching these feeding fish at sea comparatively easy, the golden days of summer rod fishing had arrived. But a price was paid for this. It was the disappearance, in all save one or two special cases, of the autumn run. The rivers could rear and support only a certain number of alevins, parr and smolts. Those deriving from the upper stretches took all the available food. Nothing was left for those hatched in the lower river. It was the end of the great autumn runs.

Today all that is left for autumn fishing in most of the great Scottish east coast rivers are the now rapidly reddening and maturing remnants of the spring and summer runs and a few very early spring fish, not due to breed until the following winter.

Nevertheless there are one or two exceptions and, of these, the big late August and September runs into the lower Tay are the most notable. These are true autumn fish, very sexually mature, the males already with big kypes on the lower jaw and both sexes full of spawn. They will lay and fertilize their eggs in the current winter. The late November runs into the Tweed are not, in the main, autumn fish at all. Except for a few caught almost in the estuary, most are very early spring fish.

The autumn fishing in the Tay (that at Islamouth is possibly the most sought-after and most expensive fishing in Britain), is for fish which are not really Tay fish at all. These true autumn runs are made up of spawners which come from and are returning to the two big tributaries, the Almond and the Isla. Both of these streams have no spring and few summer fish. As a result they can carry a large stock of late, true autumn fish.

From the point of view of the angler both the true autumn fish and the very early spring fish which enter the river, often together, are exceptionally good 'taking' fish. The early springer, fresh in from the sea and on the move until it settles down in the pool where it will spend the winter is, though toothless, still the hunter and feeder that it has been all its life. The other,

Slop an Roan at Tulchan on the River Spey. Not a great holding pool but typical of the rather shallow streamy resting pools of the middle Spey which yield a high proportion of the bag.

the sexually mature breeding fish with its aggressive colouration and its fearsome array of teeth is ready to attack all potential rivals for, in the case of the females, the choicest locations for the redds; for the males, other male fish and even well grown parr which might attempt to fertilize the eggs of his chosen mate. It is for this reason, as we shall see later, that the little greased-line flies of summer give way to the two inch and bigger flies with which the angler fishes in the autumn. We may well ask ourselves why these runs of fish should be more inclined to take a fly or bait than fish which enter in the late spring or early summer.

The late autumn run fish tends to arrive in the brackish water of the estuary in a partially advanced state of sexual maturity and is in a great hurry to get to its chosen predetermined spawning area. The spring or summer fish which has made its way in easy stages to the headwaters is in an even more advanced state of maturity. It has already completely lost its migratory dress. The male is tartan-hued. The female is the dirty-grey which has replaced the rainbow and white of her sea dress and she is turning red. In both, roe now forms a large percentage of their body weight. In males, the kype on the lower jaw is pronounced. The fish which has been in the river for several months may well have already grown an array of breeding teeth to replace the feeding teeth which were lost on leaving the pelagic feeding grounds. Time is no longer on the side of such fish. There remain, at best, but a few weeks to complete the maturing of the roe and the skeletal changes which accompany the transference of body tissues to the roe. (These are brought about by an inability to dispose of the waste products of the transfer except by depositing them on the skull, the bones of the skeleton and on thickening the skin.)

The autumn salmon is in a hurry. It is no longer interested in the memories of hunting and feeding. Your little fly which might have tempted it in summer no longer arouses any desire to catch it. Now its only interest lies in safeguarding the next generation and ensuring the survival of its own genes. Both male and female are prepared to fight off, if necessary, all competitors for the best spawning places, and all other males be they only large parr who might fertilize the eggs. Red, ugly, deformed late autumn salmon can be caught with practically anything in the way of a bait. It is not particular. It is not a simulation of a known prey which it is hunting, but a potential rival on the spawning beds.

So the problems facing the angler in the late autumn are of easy solution. There is no point in fishing the small greased-line flies of summer, though they will probably be quite successful in a clean river in the earlier days of autumn. Better by far is to use quite large flies, at least about two inches, which the breeding salmon can regard as competitors. The female fish sees them as possible rivals for the best locations, the males as rivals in fertilizing the eggs. The question of the colour, tone and even shape of the fly or bait will have to be considered later. For the time being it is enough to understand why it is that we are using flies and baits of a certain size at this time of year for both newly entered late running fish and also for fish which may have been in the river many months but which are now making their final progression into the upper reaches.

One feature which distinguishes these fish from salmon in spring and summer is that while the latter can afford ample time to rest in their easy progress upstream, these are in a hurry. Both late autumn fish and the salmon nearing its final goal after a long sojourn in the river, must quickly get to their spawning areas before the frosts come. The fish are anxious too, to get the spawning over and to attempt to get back to the sea.

All the fish that we have been discussing have one characteristic in common. All are, for one reason or another, fish which are either about to move, are on the move, or have just moved. In salmon, movement implies being both awake and in the mood to hunt.

Return to the River – the Fast Begins

Before leaving our look at the fish there are one or two special points which can materially affect the way in which we attempt to catch salmon. One is easily and quickly dealt with. I do not believe that anyone will, nowadays, argue that mature salmon can, or do, feed in fresh water. Before leaving their feeding grounds and facing a return journey of more than a thousand miles their intestines have atrophied and they have lost their teeth. For the fisherman this is important because it means that the fish is not hungry. It cannot, therefore, be tempted with food to assuage its hunger!

Before the main feeding grounds in the Denmark Strait off Greenland were discovered it was believed that the salmon fed its way slowly along the edge of the North Atlantic Drift into the Gulf Stream and returned to the river of its birth by following the same route in reverse. The whole of this return journey would take about eighteen months in the case of most salmon, but only about a year in the case of the grilse, and, perhaps up to three years in the case of some of the bigger fish. Now, however, we know that the smolt, which could not travel such a distance without food to sustain it, makes its way comparatively slowly, catching any suitable food it enounters, to its Denmark Strait feeding ground. It uses newly acquired migratory feeding teeth to catch any suitable food it encounters on the way.

It has been suggested that much of the smolt's sea food can be found in the endless stream of elvers which, hatched in the Sargasso Sea, are following the Gulf Stream round the Atlantic on their three-year journey into European and British rivers. This may well be the case. The leptocephali (or the leaf-like young elvers) which abound in the Gulf Stream and the North Atlantic Drift are virtually immobile, easily caught and very nourishing.

The now mature salmon's return journey, by contrast, is made by swift swimming and determination and is accomplished without delay. Whenever the fish feels (and no one knows what triggers this feeling) that it has stored up sufficient energy in the muscle and fat of its body, its feeding teeth drop out and its stomach ceases to secrete the gastric juices of digestion and begins to atrophy. Judging from the growth of the new breeding teeth which start to grow as soon as the feeding teeth are cast, most adult salmon make the return journey in the matter of days rather than weeks. On arrival at the river mouth these teeth are usually still not attached to the fish's jaw but are lying loosely in the membrane covering it. Very shortly they become firmly attached to the bone of the jaws and the vomer and will protrude their points through the membrane. The salmon could now become a hunting and feeding fish again. But...

It is important for the angler to understand the extraordinary situation which now develops. The fish's dentition reverts from a set of migratory or feeding teeth to a new set which would originally have developed into a set of freshwater feeding teeth in the entirely freshwater-living ancestors of the salmon (who acquired a sea-going habit only to secure better feeding). Now, however, the returned fish develops teeth suitable for hunting and feeding but is incapable of feeding and indeed can only use this very formidable array for perhaps fighting on the spawning beds. But the fact remains that these teeth are there and, in certain stages of development, may remind the fish that it has been a hunter all its days. It may well be that, when allied to circumstances which engender movement in an otherwise dormant and static fish, the reaction to the presence of something which resembles the sort of prey it might be expecting to see may provoke, or re-awaken the instinct to attack and seize the prey. Though it can in no sense eat it, the inborn desire to attack may predominate. It is this inborn desire to attack alone that enables the angler to catch a salmon . . . or, if you prefer, and more accurately, to be caught by it.

It is perhaps worth noting, *en passant*, that were it not for the proviso made by nature that mature salmon cannot eat, and therefore have no reason to hunt in fresh water, the species would have ceased to exist. And not only would salmon have disappeared, but almost every living thing in the river. Imagine if you will, a river like the Aberdeenshire Dee into which about 15,000 fish make their way every year after the nets have taken their toll. If these were all feeding fish – feeding in the manner which has allowed them to grow from a few ounces in weight to many pounds in about a year and a half, what can one suppose would happen to all the living things in the river. Not a parr, not a smolt, not a trout – no living thing would be left unkilled and uneaten. The river would be lifeless in one season.

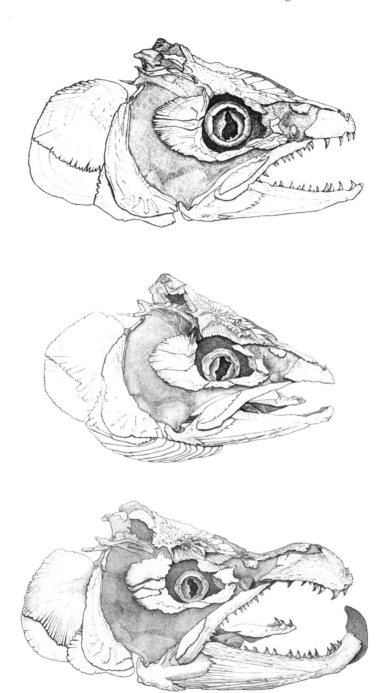

The Salmon's skull in various stages.

We have seen the problem faced by the descending smolt when it hits the salt water resulting from the differences in the salinity of its body fluids compared with those of the sea. The smolt must literally guard against, drying out if the impermeable membrane which is its skin becomes damaged. Already it has had to adjust its kidney function to filter out the salt from the sea water which it has to drink to replace the body fluid it loses by osmosis through the gills. A further loss through injury to its skin might prove fatal.

The returning salmon, finding itself in fresh water, faces the same problem, but in reverse. Its danger stems from the fact that the fluids in its body cells are more saline than the medium in which it now finds itself. Osmotic pressure forces water into the bloodstream of the salmon through its gills. If it does not excrete water it is in danger of becoming waterlogged. Any injury to its skin or to the mucous membranes of its mouth and throat aggravate this danger. In the ordinary way the salmon appears to overcome this problem without difficulty. It needs to drink salt water while in the sea to prevent itself drying out. It needs to excrete excess water while in the river to prevent itself becoming waterlogged.

This problem faces all fresh running salmon in ways which are not, at first, apparent and affects the fisherman as well. For, while it is accustoming itself to the changed conditions of a changed atmosphere, the salmon remains unsettled. It cannot, for the time being, lie quietly asleep at the bottom of a pool. It is disturbed, restless, and as such is vulnerable. It is probably for this reason that the fresh run fish can be caught so much more easily than the salmon which has been in the river for some time. Until they have accustomed themselves to the changed conditions they cannot rest and sleep. They remain awake and, accordingly, are more vulnerable than the fish which has been in freshwater long enough to have become accustomed to it. It is probable, too, that this is why a higher proportion of fish which have been injured by nets or seals seem to be more easily caught than that of unscathed salmon. These fish cannot settle down in the river in the way that the uninjured fish is able to do. Its injuries entail constant care against waterlogging. Injuries may also place great strain on the fish's kidney. This, in the salmon, is an unusually large organ which lies underneath the spine for a good two thirds of the length of the fish. It is large because it has an unusual amount of work to do. The salmon undergoes changes from an atmosphere of fresh to salt water twice, and from salt back to fresh once in its life. The tiny percentage of fish, always female, which succeed in returning from the sea a second time will undergo this change yet again. This kidney is of a very special kind not only able to filter out the salt from seawater but also to remove much of the waste which is produced by the fish when maturing sexually. It is perhaps worth noting that, large and efficient as the salmon's kidney is, it is still not able to eliminate more than a part of the waste products of the fish's metabolism. These, not excreted, are laid down on the skeleton and skin of the fish and create the changes, particularly in the skull, which so distinguish the appearance of the spawning fish from that of the fresh run salmon. It is also perhaps worth noting that the problems of elimination of waste products are more severe for the male fish than for the female and that the bigger the fish the greater the problem (as would be expected in accordance with the physical law that the surface varies as the square, and the mass as the cube, of linear dimensions). Virtually no male fish will succeed in returning to spawn a second time. A percentage, not more than five per cent of the females, all small, succeed.

We have noted that on leaving its ocean feeding grounds the salmon casts its feeding teeth and that a new set of breeding teeth start form as it approaches the river. Vestigial at first, these teeth soon become attached to the bone and continue to grow throughout the summer and autumn. By the time the salmon spawns its river teeth, especially in the males, present a formidable array. Yet this fish does not hunt and does not eat. Of what possible use are these teeth? It would seem that the fish is armed in this manner for the sole purpose of fighting off other fish threatening the chosen spawning area. These will usually be other males attempting to fertilize the eggs laid by the female in the redds and, also much more important from the angler's point of view, trout which eat the thousands of eggs which fail to find lodges in the redds and are washed downstream. As soon as spawning is finished and when the fish starts making its way back to the sea, it begins to lose these teeth and to replace them once more with a set of migratory feeding teeth.

For the angler who fishes for late autumn salmon this is of significant interest. He gives up all thoughts of tempting the fish with morsels which may represent the fish's normal prey. Instead of tiny baits and small greased-line flies, he now fishes with lures which may represent potential enemies which the salmon must attack, seize or drive off. Consequently he uses flies or baits of at least two inches in length which are best fished not too near the surface. They are about the largest which can be cast easily with the rods and tackle used for summer fishing. I have no doubt that larger flies and baits such as are used for early spring fishing would prove equally, if not more, effective.

Both male and female fish go through a form of fighting at the spawning beds. The females fight off others from chosen sites for their redd. The males fight off others, including even parr at times, who attempt to fertilize the eggs laid by the female. It is this tendency towards fighting which probably makes the late autumn fish so much easier to catch than those of spring and summer. And it can only be as an arm to fight with that the salmon grows such a formidable array of breeding teeth. It is possibly for the same reason that the autumn fish assumes a very thickened skin and a protective layer of mucous. Always susceptible to the consequences of injuries to its skin, the very thin-skinned fresh run salmon changes this garment as the season progresses into a covering which will withstand the tussles and knocks sustained on the spawning beds. The multicoloured skin of the spawning salmon can, incidentally, be tanned and makes an attractive covering, for instance for, a book!

What Can the Fish See?

Coarse fishermen, trout anglers too, tempt their prey by offering food. To the salmon, food as such, is meaningless. To tempt him it must be some memory of hunting that the fisherman tries to recall. It is on something that the fish sees that the angler must concentrate.

What and how does the salmon see? What sort of an eye has it got? The diagram gives a fair indication of the very simple and rather inefficient eye of the salmon. As an optical instrument it is very second rate. The image cast on the retina is certainly out of focus and probably distorted. There will be very poor definition of detail and though received over a large area the sensitivity to movement will be more acute than to variations in shape or even size. There appears to be no reason why the fish should be insensitive to colour. Indeed the eye is amply equipped to receive and distinguish between colours. The question is, not whether the eye can do so, but whether the fish's brain can interpret what the eye signals.

I think that most fishermen know that the fish sees through the surface of the water through a hole which extends at an angle of about 48 degrees all around him. Beyond this the surface acts like a mirror through which he cannot see and which reflects only the bottom of the river and anything growing or swimming above it. Stated in this manner it might appear that the fish is living in a 'cone' of bright light surrounded by an infinity of darkness. Nothing is further from the truth. Every point in the river is illuminated by light entering through its own cone. Consequently the river bed is fully illuminated as is everything growing or moving in the river. It follows, too, that everything in the river which is outside the cone of the fish's vision is more easily seen in reflection from the surface than directly, since it is the top of such an object which is illuminated and which is reflected. It is seen against the background of the reflected river bottom.

36

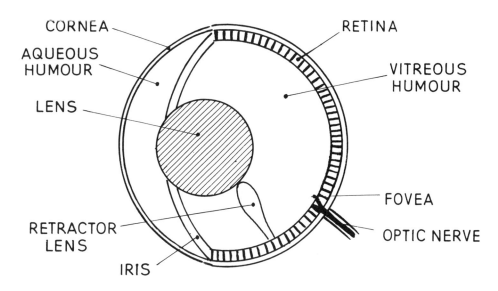

The Salmon's eye.

For the fisherman choosing his fly or bait these physical facts should, whether he realizes it or not, properly be the main influences in determining the colour, size and tone of the lure he chooses. Once the bait is observed from below and within the cone of direct light, colour, tone, and even shape, cease to be of importance. It is merely a black object seen against a very bright light. But observed while still outside the cone, where the fish will normally first see it, the bait must conform in tone, shape, size and perhaps colour to whatever the fish is accustomed to look for in its prey when judged against the tone and colour of the river bed. The old adage 'a bright fly for a bright day' is palpably bad advice when examined critically. It will be the backs of any small fish or copepod which will be seen in reflection while outside the cone. These are invariably dark or neutral in tone. Seen against either a dark or light coloured river bottom they will appear dark. And the brighter the day the more illuminated will be the river bottom against which the dark back of any little fish will be seen. It is only here, before the fly or bait swings into the fish's cone that he is able to assess whether it is worth attacking. Once in the cone it becomes shapeless, toneless and colourless. The fish must commit himself to taking before the lure swings into the cone – while it can still judge what it is that it is attacking.

It is worth noting here the error that many fly-fishers, out in the late evening, are prone to make. They tend to put on bigger and brighter flies assuming that the fish will see them more easily than dull coloured normal sized flies. This, of course, is the reverse of the truth. Because they are no longer blinded by strong sunlight the unprotected lidless eyes of the salmon can see much better in the dull conditions of fading light. The background, the river bottom, against which the fly is first observed will also be darker in tone; so, too, must the fly be even darker.

Since the last year and more of the salmon's life has been spent feeding and hunting at sea we must consider how the totally different surroundings of the deep ocean may affect its methods of catching its prey. First and foremost is the fact that in the sea the aqueous humour and other constituents of the salmon's eye are in a medium of different refractive power from that of fresh water. On entering the salt water the fish must adjust its primitive focusing arrangements to compensate for this. On returning to fresh water the reverse process is required. In the river the fish is aware at all times of the bottom. It is against the brightly- or dimly-lit reflection of the bottom that the fish observes all that is going on around it. In the sea the area outside its cone has no bottom. The surface reflects only darkness and everything which moves within sight of the fish in that area appears very brightly lit in comparison. A further consideration, of great importance to the angler, is that in the river the fish is forced to face

Shepherd's Pool on the River Carron.

38

upstream and relies on the stream to assist in its breathing. In the sea, though perhaps living in an ocean current, there is no way that it can be aware of it, and it can face any way it pleases. This is of importance to a creature with lidless eyes in a sunlit world. With the sun overhead or casting its rays straight downstream, the fish can be literally blinded when in the river. In the sea it has only to turn around and face another direction.

We have emphasized the importance of the cone of light by which the fish can see through the surface of the water and of the reflective properties of the remainder of the surface. It must be pointed out, however, that while these phenomena are of great importance to the fish in the river – and therefore to the fisherman – they may have little bearing on the way the fish behaves in the ocean.

By and large it is true to say that the salmon's sea food falls into two types. First are the small fish such as sprats and young herring or capelin which will shoal at varying depths, depending upon the temperature of the water and of the outside air. The 'sardinal' or net set by the Mediterranean fisherman, for instance, is lowered to over twenty feet under cooler conditions, but is raised almost to the surface when they become warmer. This lowering and raising of the net may occur more than once in a single day of variable temperatures. But while occasionally the 'small fish' feeding salmon may have to hunt them very near the surface, for the most part they will be taken at depths which, in the open sea, have no connection with the surface.

Second are a variety of copepods, gastropods and a few of the smaller cephalopods (shrimps, small cuttlefish, snails etc.) which inhabit the surface layers of a warmer sea. These, because they are hunted near the surface, will be looked at in reflection before they are seen directly by the feeding fish.

From the point of view of the angler the fact that the fish's ocean food falls into these two categories determines to a great extent the methods he will use in attempting to catch the salmon. We can now understand why, under certain conditions the fly-fisherman uses a sunken line and big three inch flies which fish deep in the water and well away from the surface, and, when conditions are different, may use a floating line and little flies which fish only a few inches under the surface.

To hunt and feed the salmon must rely on seeing its prey. We have shown that though the eye with which it has been endowed may leave much to be desired as an optical instrument it is, nevertheless, adequate for the fish's needs. Indeed, though inaccurate in focusing and unable to determine the detail of its objective, it has a wide range of vision with a good area of binocular vision and only a very small region behind the tail which is blind.

Compared to that of mammals and birds the eyesight of the salmon is

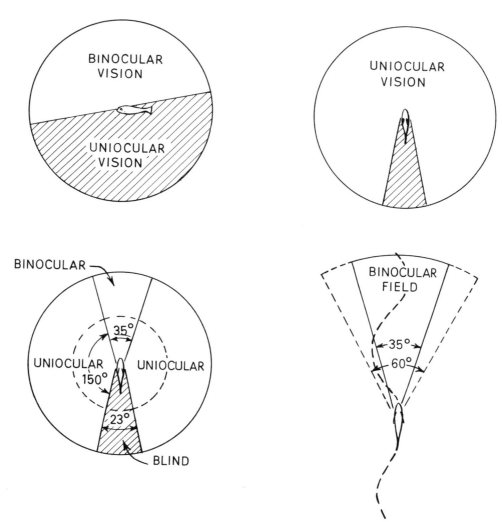

The fish's uniocular and binocular sight.

primitive and inefficient. Even if the lens adjustment mechanism works moderately well the retina upon which the lens casts the image is very inferior. It has no especially sensitive area in the centre and is evenly covered with 'rods' and 'cones'. This eye can discern movement over a wide angle (about 150 degrees). It can 'see' the general size, shape and colour of an object, but little of its minor detail. Only in the small area of about 35 degrees in front of and above its head in which it has binocular vision can the salmon's sight be regarded by a mammal, such as ourselves, as even reasonable.

But, and this is a very big 'but', what the salmon's eye sees and what the fish's tiny brain accepts are two entirely different matters. The eye, like a camera lens, 'sees' everything to which it is exposed. Your eye and mine does this also. Like the camera lens, the lens of the eye passes the light from everything to which it is exposed, even in a flash, to the retina. But man's brain is unable to accept and record even a thousandth part of the detail which the eyes have seen. Even if we look at an object for several seconds our minds still cannot accept much of the detail of what our eye has seen. If this is the best that we can do, what do you suppose that the fish's brain can accept in the way of the detail of a fly or bait which is exposed to its vision only as it moves across the stream? Our fish, then, can see somewhat indifferently with a rather second-rate eye. It is very sensitive to movement of anything over a wide range but quite insensitive to the detail of an object. Its eye probably 'sees' colour but its brain disregards it and is not too particular about tone. Both visually and intellectually the fish's eye and brain cannot differentiate between the niceties of small differences in the size of objects. The thinking fisherman will have regard to all these facts when choosing his way of fishing and the baits or flies which he will use.

On a fine early summer morning the angler who sets out for his day's fishing has no problems about the methods which he is going to use. The river is running at a perfect fishing height, the light is good, and the air feels warm. His is a good beat that day and the top pool where he is going to start lies immediately below a bridge – the Blacksboat Bridge over the river Spey at Pitchroy. His ghillie has met him on the bridge and suggests that he spends a few minutes looking at the fish in the pool below.

The fisherman, having looked over the bridge and seen a great number of salmon lying all the length of the pool, decides to fish it down with his fly. His ghillie, watching from the bridge can see both the fly and the fish and is disappointed when not only is no fish caught, but no fish has even moved to, or taken any notice of the fly. 'They are all asleep' he calls to the fisherman. 'No' replies the latter, 'they are just not taking'. Who do you think is right?

I am sure, now, that it was the ghillie. I think that when he described the fish as being 'asleep' he was giving an accurate description of the state in which he observed them. As a fisherman I tend to regard the salmon in a pool as being awake and 'looking' at all times. After all, it cannot close those lidless eyes. But I am wrong. To survive, the salmon must enjoy some form of sleep. Since it cannot close its eyes it must be able to 'turn off' what its eyes see from registering in its brain. In short, the fish cannot help 'looking' but its brain prevents its 'seeing'.

If we now adopt the perfectly plausible view that virtually all the fish lying in a pool are 'turned off' or asleep, then we have a very reasonable answer to the query: 'why do they all ignore all forms of fly or bait presented to them?' In 'sleep' they are preserving the energy stored in their body tissues in the only way open to them. This has not only to last them for many months without replacement, but has also to take them on many long miles of upstream swimming followed by the exhaustion of spawning and the long, long return journey to salt water again. The conservation of energy must be the prime consideration in determining the salmon's behaviour during its fast in freshwater. What then causes an occasional fish in an unguarded moment to remember its hunting days? Why, out of perhaps several hundred salmon in a pool are there sometimes none that can be moved by the fisherman, at other times possibly only one, occasionally two or more? The thinking fisherman will seek an answer to these questions and will not be satisfied until such an answer allows him to fish in a rational manner. That the answer may be totally incorrect does not matter. What is important is that the angler finds a reason which satisfies him for everything he does. Otherwise salmon fishing becomes what the trivial trout fisherman contemptuously describes as 'chuck and chance it' fishing.

What, then, can awaken one fish out of perhaps many hundreds in a pool? Why does this one fish decide to take while the remainder affect complete indifference to your fly? I think that an answer, if not *the* answer, is that this one sleeping fish has been wakened, not by your fly, but by some other influence or change in its surroundings which, like a rise in the river, may well have aroused most of the fish, but only one or two of them sufficiently to consider the resumption of hunting.

Is Colour Important?

If the only taking fish in the pool is to be caught it can only be because it has been tempted to attack something which resembles the prey that it would expect to see under similar circumstances during its feeding life, either as a parr or smolt in the river or as a feeding fish in the sea. Fortunately for the angler the salmon's eyesight is so poor that, while aware of size and speed of movement, it can mistake such a monstrosity as a 8/0 fly for a fish. That its eye can 'see' colour is certain. The retina is equally endowed with both rods and cones and is receptive to colour. The question is not whether it can distinguish one colour from another, but whether, in fact, it does so.

The question of whether a fish sees in colour has bothered fishermen, both trout, salmon and coarse anglers for generations. Sir Herbert Maxwell, in the early days of the century, proved, as he thought, that trout could not distinguish one colour from another. He caught up a number of Mayflies, dyed some of them blue, some red and left others natural. Released in the river he noted that feeding trout made no distinction between either of the colours and ate them as readily as the natural. Some years later Dr J. C. Mottram, a scientist who looked at the fish eye as an optical instrument decided that there was no reason why fish, in general, should not be able to distinguish one colour from another. He quite correctly pointed out that the Maxwell experiment really told nothing. Seen against a bright sky by a rising trout, all the Mayflies would appear the same . . . black! Furthermore, suppose the fish could distinguish the colours, why should the fact that a fly was coloured prevent it from being eaten? The fish associated no danger from it.

So Mottram devised an experiment which would prove that a fish could distinguish between one colour and another. He took a roach and trained it, first, to choose between red and white pellets of food. These pellets were attached to cotton and were lowered into the fish's tank. Every time the fish made to take a red pellet it was pulled away from it. After 'six weeks daily training' to use Mottram's own words, 'the fish had come to realize that the red pellet was no good to her and so, never attempted to take it.' When blue pellets were substituted for white, the fish took them, but never the red. In three months the fish never attempted to take a red pellet even though no others were offered. Finally some purple (mixture of red and blue) pellets were offered. The fish became very confused and after a few abortive attempts to take one of these eventually gave up and refused. This fish, with the same sort of eye as the salmon, most certainly was not colour-blind. Nor, do I believe, is the salmon itself. Nevertheless, though all the evidence points to the fact that the fish's eye is fully equipped to see and distinguish between colours, is the salmon's brain either able or willing to accept the signals received from its eye? This is the question which we must answer if we are to fish in a rational manner.

When I was the tenant of the Inverness-shire Garry that I first began to wonder whether it was not somewhat nonsensical to concern myself over the colours of the feathers and dressing in the flies which I was using. After all none of them looked like anything in nature and to suppose that a fish with such rotten vision were able to distinguish between, say, a Logie and a Jenny, or if able, would want to, seemed absurd. The Garry flowing out of the loch was always very clear and clean, even in spates. There was one pool, the

Fishing from the Pulpit in the Chest Pool.

44

Chest which was fished off a 'pulpit'. Casting from this I could see not only my fly in the water, but also the fish lying in a channel between two big rocks. I was interested in the way in which a rather small dark fly, a No 6 Blue Charm I recall, moved across the lie and seemed to excite a fish. In order to get a better look at the way the fly was fishing I changed the Blue Charm for a Garry Dog, bright yellow, and cast again. Once or twice the fish moved to it but did not take. But when I cast less squarely across the stream and by mending managed to hang the fly momentarily in front of the fish's nose it at once rose up and took it. I would agree that there is nothing very remarkable about this almost everyday account of hooking a salmon. Yet this one incident profoundly affected all my salmon fishing for the rest of my days. Why, you may ask? Simply because of that bright yellow fly!

If we are going to accept that it is force of habit acquired from years of hunting and eating that induces the fish, now 'un-hungry' and incapable of utilizing any food, to attack the fly or bait which reminds it of the food which it used to enjoy, then the stimulus is the message carried from its eye to its brain. The salmon's eye, like a somewhat indifferent camera, sees everything within its scope. But what the eye sees and what the brain interprets from the signal is, as we have already noted, quite another matter. The feeding parr, the smolt and the pelagic salmon are, almost without exception, catching food which is neutral in shade and certainly not highly coloured. Why, then, does the fisherman choose to use such highly coloured lures to catch the fish? I think, now, that because the unknown, the mystery and magic are a great part of the fascination which salmon fishing exerts over its devotees, much of the pleasure lies in pondering over the possible effects which a change in the colour of fly or bait might have upon the fish's willingness to take. Nevertheless I must most regretfully state that it is definitely my opinion that while the fish's eye can certainly see colour, its brain is either incapable of differentiating between colours or is completely indifferent to colour. I firmly believe that this failure to recognise colour is absolute and that, consequently, it does not matter in the very least what colour of fly or bait you care to fish with.

The prawn fisherman will disagree with me. His chosen bait is the boiled prawn and he will argue that it is the redness which is largely responsible for attracting the fish. The spinning prawn is nothing other than a very untidy and shapeless minnow. Fished Irish fashion, sink and draw, it looks and moves like a prawn: but though there are occasional reddish crustaceans in the sea most uncooked prawns and shrimps have a rather muddy greenish and slightly transparent look and when attacked, swim backwards – about as unlike a boiled spinning prawn as could be imagined. Yet the salmon will readily go for these monstrosities and completely disregard their colour.

During my lifetime the fashion in the colours of both flies and baits has changed very markedly. While still a student I was lucky enough to be allowed to fish the famous Saugh Pool of the Aberdeenshire Don. This pool, which I remember being netted on the 11 February 1927 and yielding some five or six hundred fish on the first draw of the net, was perhaps the most prolific of the spring pools of the lower Don. Davidson's paper mill which owned the right bank (the best for fishing) employed a pensioner, Donald Grant, to fish it for them giving him a percentage of the catch. The lower Don in those days never ran other than fairly or very dirty since all the washings from the mills as far away as Inverurie were carried by it. Yet, except in the very dirtiest spates the only bait ever used was a natural sand eel, uncoloured. Grant, of course knew every stone in the bottom and every lie throughout the pool suitable for every height of water. I do not know of any salmon pool which was fished more thoroughly and more expertly than the Saugh. No thought of using any coloured bait ever crossed anyone's mind and I am quite certain that the rod catch could never have been improved by the use of any bait with colour. Nowadays no bait fisherman considers himself equipped unless he has lures of every hue of the rainbow in his bait box. The one most used, often a Golden Sprat, is the one which last caught a fish, only to be changed after a prolonged and unsuccessful trial. If a blue or a red bait is tried and is successful it will take the place of the golden until it, too, is discarded. It is the same with flies. The moment a fish is caught on, say a Lady Caroline, all the Spey fishermen within range are fishing this pattern. I may add that my normally fishing a Yellow Torrish or a Garry Dog has many followers who have noted that these patterns are, if no better, certainly no worse at attracting fish and it is often fun to be able to see them in the water while fishing.

Whereas not everyone will concede that colour is unimportant, I am sure that all will agree that both tone and shape must conform in principle to what the salmon might be hunting, and that its size, and, more important, the way it moves, are the vital properties of the successful lure. Fortunately, as mentioned before, its eyesight is so poor that it can mistake such a monstrosity as an 8/0 fly for a fish! The basic problem remains unanswered. Why does a creature which cannot eat ever behave as if it was hunting food? And, more specifically, why does it, for the greater part of its river life take no notice of possible food but suddenly not only takes notice, but attacks a supposed prey?

If we are to fish in a rational manner we must have an answer to this problem. Every thinking fisherman has his own answers. All will be different. Mine, based on my own experiences, are clear. I can recall days, prior to the war, when in low water all fishing seemed to come to a standstill,

The Saugh pool at Mugiemoss on the River Don.

and when the numbers of salmon in the good pools of the Aberdeenshire Dee could be reckoned in hundreds if not thousands, yet not a fish could be caught by any legal means. I remember the Irrigation Pool at Aboyne so full of uncatchable fish already turning red in the month of March that the bottom of the pool looked black. And I remember taking out four fish with a 3in fly, two of which were foul-hooked and the others, to my ghillie's immense surprise, taken by the mouth. I recall, too, a day when fishing Spearnick on the then 'B' beat of Tulchan. No one could touch a fish though there were a number in the pool on that May morning. Four of us each had a go with flies and baits of every sort . . . nothing! Then my chauffeur arrived bringing a young lady from the train. She was interviewing for a possible job as secretary. 'Have you ever fished?' I asked her, 'Yes' she answered, 'I caught a pike in Ireland.' So I gave her a spinning rod and told her to cast. The result was awful. While sorting out the tangle the bait sank to the bottom. As she reeled in she announced 'I think I have caught a fish.' She certainly had. Janet Ashton, now about the best salmon fisherman of her sex in the country landed a fourteen pound fish; her first, and surprise, surprise, it had taken the bait properly and was hooked in the mouth. I recall, too, another lady fishing with a small spinner in a deep pool opposite Kylnadrochit Lodge on the Aven and allowing it to sink to the bottom where two or three fish were lying dormant. No one had induced any of these fish even to move to any bait. But as Kathie lifted her bait from beside a fish it quietly turned round and took it.

Spearnick – a perfect salmon pool on the River Spey. Lord Alanbrook fishing the stream.

Consider, too, the problem posed by worm fishing. When the salmon will look at nothing else they will frequently very readily take a worm. Indeed I have noticed that even in some of the best beats of the Wye many fishermen use nothing else. I have given a great deal of thought to these problems in a long fishing lifetime and, as must every thinking fisherman, I have arrived at answers which satisfy me but, possibly, no one else. I consider that though the salmon cannot and does not eat in freshwater, on its return from several months of hunting and feeding in the sea, the desire to attack and kill food remains, albeit dormant, with it. But faced with a sojourn of many months of fasting and the expenditure of a lot of energy in reaching its spawning area the conservation of its stored resources is of paramount importance. I am sure that, when not actively engaged in running, or preparing to run, the salmon literally sleeps. Though its eye is open (because it cannot close it) it does not see, and what it does not see cannot recall the days of hunting. The odd taking fish, often just one out of many hundreds, may have been awakened by some external influence. A change in the river level may arouse

*Torrans pool on the River A'an (Aven) which is a main tributary of
the Spey, with Kylnadrochit (The House by the Bridge) in the
background. Torrans is a very good fly pool at all heights.*

a number. Perhaps a warming sun has broken through the clouds on a cold
day. Possibly a storm of rain has altered the acidity of the river water. Even a
hatch of grannom flies has disturbed the salmon. But the reason that the
occasional fish is caught by baits which have sunk to the bottom and by
worms which are fished among resting fish is that, though asleep, the fish is
partly awakened by, possibly, the bait touching it and, awakened, is now
vulnerable. I have found this philosophy as good a basis as any other upon
which to practise my methods of fishing. I think every angler should think
out his own. '*Quot homines . . .*'

The Right Rods for Modern Fishing

In recent years many changes have occurred, not only in salmon fishing methods, but also in the tackle and rods used.

There can be little doubt that the modern salmon rod is an infinitely better instrument than those we fished with in my younger days. It has taken the better part of the century to complete a turn-around from the very long rods of the early days, through a number of years when anglers fished for salmon with rods that were uncomfortably short (and consequently too heavy and powerful), to the modern fashion of using sensibly long, light, and easily handled rods. These are made from modern materials which impart adequate strength without unnecessary weight.

In Victorian and Edwardian times the 18ft Greenheart, or the Washaba or Hickory of up to 20ft was fished as standard by both 'gentlemen' and ghillies. So heavy and clumsy were these in overhead casting that all sorts of 'Spey' and 'roll' casts were invented to relieve the strain of fishing these heavy lines and big flies. I often think that the reason that bait fishing became popular at this time was because of the enormous effort required in fly-casting and the difficulty that even experienced fishermen encountered in learning to 'Spey' cast. For some years, between the wars, fashion in fishing dictated a change to shorter, but more powerful, rods. By the thirties a salmon rod of more than 14ft 6in was practically never seen. I still have a 16ft Greenheart which I acquired specially to fish the Aaro river with Nicolai Denisoff but which would have made my Spey ghillie think I had gone mad if I had asked him to put it up for me on that river. Most of us in Scotland fished with 'Grant Vibration' Greenhearts which were heavier than Hardy or Sharp split cane rods but which 'Spey' cast rather more easily. The trouble with all

Greenheart or Washaba rods was that, used properly with the heavy line which was required when fishing 8/0 flies, it was inevitable that they broke, usually in the middle joint of a three-piece rod. I have a feeling that it may have been the influence that Arthur Wood of Cairnton had on fishing that caused this change from heavy to over-short rods. A big powerful man who fished a beat of the Dee where all the catchable fish could be reached very easily off the numerous jetties, he often liked to fish with a single-handed 12ft rod. Because much of the Dee can be fished with a trout rod in any event, Arthur Wood's example of fishing with a 12ft rod became popular. But, of course few were strong enough to fish this single-handed, so the rod-makers built powerful rods of this length which were to be used double-handed. By the beginning of the Second World War it was not uncommon to see early spring 3in flies being fished from rods only 12ft in length. I remember very clearly being lent such a rod by the late Graeme Whitelaw when fishing Pitchroy on the Spey. Fortunately I was, at that time, in the best of physical condition. I needed to be. That rod was immensely powerful and threw a beautiful long line. But it required very strong, fit, arms to make it work.

This was true of all the better 12ft rods which were in common use at the time. Arthur Wood himself fished mostly single-handed and, as I remember, with split cane rods. He never needed to cast a long line or to 'Spey' cast at Cairnton. On the whole 12ft double-handed rods, even those only powerful enough to fish the greased-line and small flies, needed too much effort for

Aberlour on the River Spey with a distillery in the background.

the average fisherman. Light whippy ones which had to be fitted with very light lines were impracticable in any sort of wind. It was inevitably the fate of all lady anglers to be given light 12ft rods. The heavier and better rods required more effort than most ladies could manage and so they were fitted out with rods which, except in the calmest conditions, could cast scarcely as much line as would cover the stream.

How different are things today. The invention of the carbon fibre rod has altered the whole concept of fly-fishing for many men and for all ladies.

The first noticeable change, as we have noted, is in the length of the rods now generally used. When weight is no longer a consideration fishermen have decided that much longer rods can achieve the distance required with less effort. The long rod also allows greater control of the line and fly. At last ladies can use the new light carbon fibre rods of 15 and 16ft and can compete with their menfolk both as fly-casters and as fishermen.

The beauty, too, of these rods is that they can be manufactured to be as powerful as may be required by the fishermen. The range is enormous, from the sloppy and weak to the stiffened competition casting rod; and they can be made stiff or supple in any part to suit the preference of the individual. I, personally, find it difficult to understand why anyone should, today, wish to acquire a Greenheart or even a split cane when by paying a little more they can have a carbon fibre rod. Nevertheless there remain many, like myself, who, I must confess, continue to use the old friendly split cane of days when a rod of 14ft 6in was considered big. It is only when I am lent one of the new rods that I realise how much easier it is to fish with and, especially, how much less effort it requires to cast a given length of line both overhead and 'Spey' or switch casting.

Ideally the complete salmon angler is equipped with four rods. For spring fishing with a sunk line casting 8/0 flies he needs a 16 to 17ft rod of as much power as he can reasonably fish with all day. For bigger rivers which often require long lines, for greased-line, floating line, and fishing with small summer flies, a less powerful rod of between 15 and 16ft is needed. For fishing small flies, either on floating or sunk lines in smaller rivers a single-handed rod of about 11ft 6in is ideal. This rod also fulfils a further need. It is the perfect rod for fishing the upstream worm for salmon (and sea trout) in low water.

Besides the three fly rods the complete angler for salmon requires a spinning rod. This can be anything from about 8ft to 12ft in length depending upon the type of river fished (big rivers like the Tay need long casts and a longer rod) and the kind of spinning reel used. Very little rivers can be fished easily and most conveniently with tiny rods of not more than 4 or 5ft when very small baits are to be cast. Again, Greenheart rods, while

The River Tamar, with Conrad Voss Bach casting.

53

perfectly satisfactory for casting, are too easily broken especially when trying to clear a snagged bait. Split cane rods are probably the most satisfactory, but excellent fibreglass rods are now manufactured and are sold very cheaply. Of course carbon fibre rods, too, cannot be faulted save on the matter of needless expense.

I have found, in general, that rod-makers tend to be influenced too much by the demands of competition fishermen who require a special type of rod for long casting. These competition rods are needlessly powerful in the butt section and need great physical strength to get them to work properly. They are most tiring to fish with and often seem very clumsy and insensitive. To fly-fish in maximum comfort the angler needs a rod which does most of the work for him. By this I mean that with a level pull from the arms and hands the rod flexes along its whole length when lifting the line. It likewise flexes again when throwing the line forwards and the caster should be able to feel the movement right down to the handle. Good rods always feel a little top-heavy, and they should never have whippy tops. Since every book that has ever been written on salmon fishing repeats advice on choosing a rod, line and oddments of tackle I do not propose to add further to this. The responsible fishing tackle shop will provide all the advice necessary.

The Spring-Run Salmon

We have looked at the salmon in some detail. We have watched it grow from the eyed ova in the egg into the alevin carrying its own yolk sac. We have seen the alevin grow into a parr feeding for two or more years on the variety of insect and microscopic life which the river provides. We have noted it reaching the prescribed size in the spring and donning its migratory dress. And we have seen it disappear on a long voyage to an area of the ocean where a cold and a warm current mingle to produce a variety of foods in quantities which can be found nowhere else. We have looked at the salmon's teeth, at its eyes and at the store of energy which it carries in the fats and tissues of its muscle. We have seen that it can no longer feed once it returns to the river and must live off this store, must produce the eggs and milt from it, and retain enough to get it back to the sea. And we have opined that in order to achieve all this and at the same time grow from a fish of a few ounces to one of many pounds in weight it has had to feed continuously and voraciously throughout his pelagic existence. It is because we believe that the habit of hunting and feeding is so engrained in the fish's tiny mind that we can presume to hope that in presenting something which may remind it of a sought-after prey, it will attempt to catch it though it can no longer eat it. But it is not nearly as simple as this. The salmon shows an astonishing discrimination in choosing the type of fly or bait which sometimes awakens dormant habits and in doing so demonstrates that there is a duality in its hunting and feeding habits which the thinking fisherman must understand and to which he must correspondingly attune his methods. The salmon hunting in the cold waters of winter and spring feeds, it seems, on sizeable fish or squid which do not normally inhabit the top layer of the ocean. When fishing for salmon in the river the angler must clearly offer lures which fall within the range of size that the fish might expect to see, and must also be sure that the fly or bait swims deep enough in the water not to be confused with any reflection easily noticeable by the fish.

The river is running at normal winter height, is quite clear and, still being fed partly from melting snow, is still in the thirties Fahrenheit. A number of early fish have been in the pool for two or three weeks but a small run came in and joined them overnight. There also appears, from the rises seen in the tail, to be a few fish passing into – and probably out of the pool. The angler decides to try a fly down first.

Immediately the fisherman encounters problems and faces decisions to be made. What size of fly should he use? Fortunately he has little option. He knows that at this time of year and when the water is still cold the ocean-going salmon will be eating small fish and hunting them well away from the surface. He knows, too, that whereas flies as big as 9/0 and even 10/0 are occasionally used, 8/0 or 'three inch' flies are for practical purposes the largest which can be cast with ease from his 16ft rod. 8/0 flies give a fair representation to the fish's poor eye of a young herring or a capelin or, dare one say it, a growing smolt newly arrived in the feeding area.

Our fisherman now examines the contents of his fly-box. Acquired over a lifetime, the flies for sunk line fishing are a colourful collection of mainly 8/0, a few 9/0 and one or two smaller 5/0 and 6/0. It is a clear day, the water is clear and the sun is likely to come out at times. He wishes to fish an 8/0 fly as it requires rather too much effort to fish bigger even though the fish might prefer something really big in this cold water. But the question is 'what colour'?

To the thinking fisherman the argument that yesterday morning, under similar conditions, old Colonel Bloggs caught a fish with a three inch Mar Lodge is not a valid reason for immediately looking out a Mar Lodge from his fly-box. Instead he asks himself, 'was there any special virtue in this fly, or would any other have been equally successful?' There is no answer to this question save that which experience alone provides. For while fisherman 'A' put on his Mar Lodge and failed to move a fish, his friend 'B' preferred fishing with a less flashily dressed fly. He put on a 'Thunder and Lightning', much darker in tone, and hooked two fish first time down the pool. Immediately fisherman 'A' discarded his Mar Lodge and put on a 'Thunder and Lightning'. Poor 'A' now failed to move a fish with his new fly and was really in trouble. What should be his next move? There is no answer.

Pondering over this our thinking fisherman sits down on the bank, pulls out his pipe and reflects. The first thing which occurs to him is that not only do both flies, very different in colour from each other seem to catch or not

Spinning on the River A'an. The fisherman is in full view of the fish and will require a miracle to succeed.

catch fish equally well. He also recalls that two others from the hotel, each spinning totally different baits, one a 'Yellowbelly', the other a Norwegian spoon of about 4in, both took fish and had pulls from one or two others. Can it be that the salmon is in any sense particular about the colour or even the tone of the fly or bait used? He now remembers what he has learnt about the fish and its eye and recalls that, in its natural hunting environment, the deep sea, the salmon will be seeing prey of neutral tone and indeed, with only occasional exceptions, prey which might be termed either colourless or only black and white. Consequently colour and, unless outrageously wrong, tone, can have little meaning to the fish hunting away from the surface. The thinking fisherman now understands that the colour of the fly he fishes with, the tone even, has little effect on the salmon's willingness to take. Can it be that the way he fishes, or rather makes his fly move and fish, is what induces the salmon to attack? The more he considers this the more certain he becomes that it does not matter in the very least what colour of fly, what combination of colours, is required for a successful salmon fly. He eventually arrives at the point where, like this author, he fishes always in summertime when using the greased-line with only a bright yellow fly. Why bright yellow? Because the fisherman can often see it in the water while it is fishing and the salmon takes it quite as readily as flies of any other colour.

For the big sunk fly which will be seen by the fish directly and not in

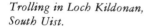

Trolling in Loch Kildonan, South Uist.

reflection from the surface it may be felt that a fairly dark fly will show up more easily in clear water and a brighter fly in coloured or dirty water. But, as far as this writer is concerned a bright yellow Garry Dog or a Torrish will do for either. The angler, in the early months of the year while the water is still cold (under about 48° F as we shall see later), is now in a situation where many of the basic problems such as the size and colour of the fly or bait he should use have been answered. Indeed, by thinking things out, he has answered them himself. The fly should be 8/0 or 9/0 in size, certainly no smaller. His rod must be big and powerful enough to cast these large flies and his line must not float as it is imperative that the fly fishes well below the surface. If he decides to use a bait it, too, must be of the right size – at least three inches in length – and it, too, must be fished well below the surface. He has also answered the problem which perhaps induces more doubt and confusion to fishermen than any others. What is the best colour or combination of colours for flies and baits? The answer is simple. It really does not matter. For the fish, even if its eye can see and distinguish colours perfectly well, takes no notice of colour. It behaves as if its brain were incapable of accepting the colour message from its eye. It appears to view life only in black and white. The thinking fisherman must do likewise. He should fish with the colour of fly or bait which pleases him. It is all the same as far as the fish is concerned. The skill in fishing lies not in the choice of fly or bait of the proper size, but in the way that it is fished.

Fly and Bait in Cold Water

Throughout the earlier part of this book we have taken a careful and detailed look at the salmon. We have postulated that astonishingly, a creature unable to feed, concerned only with the necessity of arriving at the spawning bed with as much energy conserved to support breeding and the return to the sea, should allow itself the luxury of momentarily recalling its hunting years and of attacking a supposed prey. Even more astonishing is that it does this in a medium – fresh water – which provides an 'atmosphere' requiring both physiological and physical adjustments to mind and body, the effects of which we, as land animals, cannot even begin to imagine. We are left with the hope that not only can the fish mistake the monstrosities we use as lures for the real thing, but that we can make them behave as if they were. In other words we have to learn to fish our flies and baits so that they move in a manner which little fish of that size could, and would, swim.

The first thing which the thinking fisherman must remember is that his fly or bait is seen very differently by the fish in the river from the same lure seen in the sea. The reason is that, even though hunting in the Gulf Stream, flowing at some four knots, the salmon is unaware of its movement. The prey which he is hunting is also living in the same fast moving current, and in a deep ocean there is no landmark against which the current can be measured. Very different is the case in the river. Here the salmon is not only aware of the current but utilizes it at all times. When resting, asleep(?) in a pool the current helps in holding the fish in its lie by eddying round the stones and rocks of the bottom and in sweeping water constantly over its gills. Consequently anything moving in the river has its speed of movement judged, not against the stationary stones and rocks, but against the speed of the current in which it moves. The fisherman, having cast his fly across the river watches it swing round towards his own bank and judges it to be moving at 4mph – very nice, and just about the speed that a small fish would swim – but the salmon lying in a stream running at some 5mph sees something very different. The fly is now moving at some 9mph through the water – a speed utterly impossible to so small a fish. Far from being attracted to a succulent little fish, he is suddenly frightened by an unknown creature which is probably dangerous.

The secret of success in fishing both fly and bait in cold water lies in fishing them at the right depth and at the right speed. With both achieved perfectly there is no guarantee that any fish can be awakened and persuaded to spend precious energy in attack. But if there is a 'vulnerable' awakened fish in the pool the properly fished bait has the chance of catching him. The badly fished bait which moves unnaturally has no chance at all.

During the early spring, cold water fishing months, salmon tend to lie in deeper and less streamy areas of the pool. This, I think, is really a reflection of the fact that at sea in the winter and spring months the salmon is living well away from the surface and is hunting fish which, like the sardines, shoal in deeper water in colder weather. Above all, from the fisherman's point of view, at this time of year the salmon does not hunt small fish which live in the surface layers of the ocean and which it can see most easily by looking for their reflection in the mirror of the surface.

The first question is 'What is the right depth?', and 'Is it always the same?' In the previous paragraph we have already mentioned the shoaling of sardines at different depths. If the sea is being cooled by cold air the fishermen will set the 'sardinal' net as much as twenty feet below the surface. As the day warms up so the net is raised until, in a warm afternoon, it is set just below the surface. The pelagic salmon hunting similar-sized fish will find them at depths which will vary as the temperature of the day varies. Sometimes the little fish or the copepods will be found in layers of the sea as much as thirty feet down. On a warm sunny afternoon, however, the same shoals can be hunted near the surface.

Our thinking fisherman has committed himself to the belief that the only reason that a salmon will take fly or bait, is the remembrance of hunting and feeding similar prey in the sea under varying conditions of temperature, pressure, and light. If this memory is to be wakened in the sleeping fish in a totally dissimilar environment, any condition in the sea which can be simulated or copied in fresh water must be sought. In wintertime, for instance, the salmon seeks its food in deeper water when the freezing temperatures of the far north rapidly cool the surface of the ocean. In the diminished light of a shortened day it can see little save in the 'window' above it and must swim virtually among its prey which will have also abandoned the cooling ocean surface. At what depth, then, should the fly or

The upper part of the River Beauly looking north. Some of the biggest bags ever recorded have come from the Beauly.

bait be fished? I believe that we are now approaching the heart of the matter.

Every angler who has fished in the early months of spring will recall that at the start of his day before the sun has begun to warm both the air and the river, it is very difficult to find any fish, even in the best stocked pools, which will take any interest in his fly or his bait. But allow the day to warm up and the sun to start to raise the water temperature, even only a fraction of a degree, and any taking or wakened fish begin to show interest. It may be said that this is because the fish, a cold blooded creature whose body temperature is maintained always at that of the water in which it finds itself, now wakes up to a changing condition. This may very well be the case. Far more important though will be the change in attitude undergone by the fish towards a possible prey. On a cold winter's night the salmon will be lying nose against a big stone in a quiet deep part of the pool. It is quite aware (though you may well ask how it knows this) that as the temperature drops below 36°, water which is colder than this rises so that the least cold, and likely to stay constantly warmest, part of the pool is at the bottom. Unless the angler can fish his fly or his spinner in this bottom layer of water he cannot tempt the fish who expects to find its prey on its own level. It is virtually impossible to fish a fly, however big or heavy, along the bottom of a deep pool. A bait fished deeply enough always gets hung up on rocks.

When the sun rises, or when less cold air begins to raise the temperature of the water, the fish remembers that its food begins to swim in rising levels of layers of the sea. He is no longer interested in anything at, or on, the bottom but as the day wears on, increasingly at middle and upper levels of water in the pool. This is why the experienced fisherman will wait on a cold spring morning before wading into the river. 'It's too cold now,' he may say to his ghillie 'but if the sun comes out they may start taking at lunchtime.' And until the chill of the evening descends on the river, he will know that the best chance he has is in the warmer afternoon. The angler must imagine his fish in the deepest part of the pool, aware that any natural prey will also be seeking the perhaps slightly warmer water of the deepest layers which he cannot fish properly at the start of the day.

With the sun bringing a rise in temperature the shoals move nearer and nearer to the surface. In the sea, the feeding salmon would now observe its victims beginning to swim at levels somewhat above it and would also find it easier to attack them, still not too close to the surface, when he could view them in the brightness of the 'cone' above him. Both fly and bait are more successful when the river begins to warm up. Neither fly nor bait can fish successfully along the bottom of the river bed. But in a warming river, first a heavy bait, then a big fly begin to fish well at the right depths – the depth at which the salmon would expect to see them.

*River Langa, Iceland. This photograph shows the tail of the Strengir
pool, with the Breidan pool below the bridge and the sea in the distance.*

One of the reasons that fly-fishing in the early months of the season has
given way to bait fishing in many rivers is that to fish big, heavy flies
successfully needs tackle suitable for this type of fishing, but which is
unsuitable for fly-fishing when the water is warmer. Casting 8/0 flies with a
line which is too light to carry the fly forward properly is exceedingly
uncomfortable. A line, too, which does not sink adequately prevents the fly
from sinking. The secret of success with the fly at this time of year lies in
fishing it as deeply as possible in the cold, early part of the day and as slowly
as is reasonable. It is almost impossible to fish the early spring fly at too
great a depth. Unfortunately, lifting big flies on heavy lines out of deep
water proves too tiring for a number of anglers. Many attempt to
compromise by fishing smaller flies on lighter tackle. Unless the water and
air temperature are above the normal such compromises are a waste of time
and effort. Better, by far, is to go over to the fly-fisher's enemy and use a bait
rod and spinner – suitably weighted!

For the determined fly-fisher few problems arise over the choice of fly.
The size is a minimum of 3in or 8/0. The colour is anything which the
fisherman likes to fish with – the fish certainly does not mind for all colours

1   *Murtle beat on the River Dee, now being syndicated time-share.*

2 *The author at Little Crooked pool on the River Garry.*

3 *The Dalmally beat on the River Orchy.*

4 *Success at last after a blank day.*

Published by
THE HIGHLANDS AND ISLANDS DEVELOPMENT BOARD,
Bridge House, 20 Bridge Street, Inverness IV1 1QR

THE ATLA

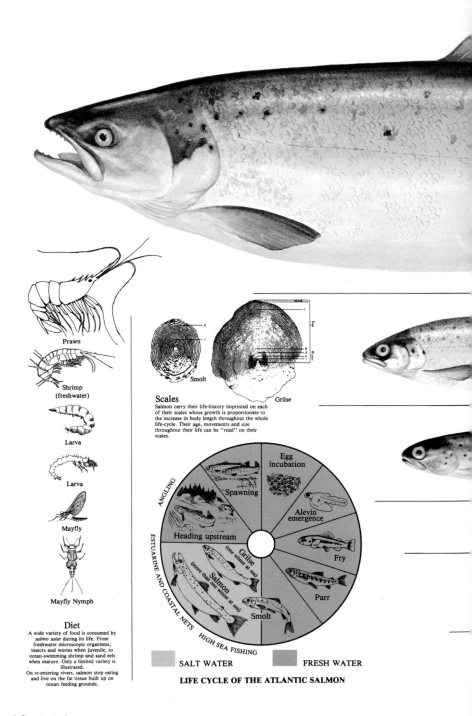

Prawn

**Shrimp
(freshwater)**

Larva

Larva

Mayfly

Mayfly Nymph

Diet
A wide variety of food is consumed by
salmo salar during its life. From
freshwater microscopic organisms,
insects and worms when juvenile, to
ocean-swimming shrimp and sand eels
when mature. Only a limited variety is
illustrated.
On re-entering rivers, salmon stop eating
and live on the fat tissue built up on
ocean feeding grounds.

Smolt

Grilse

Scales
Salmon carry their life-history imprinted on each
of their scales whose growth is proportionate to
the increase in body length throughout the whole
life-cycle. Their age, movements and size
throughout their life can be "read" on their
scales.

Egg
incubation

Spawning

Alevin
emergence

ANGLING

Heading upstream

Fry

ESTUARINE AND COASTAL NETS

Grilse
(one winter at sea)

Salmon
(more than one winter at sea)

Parr

Smolt

HIGH SEA FISHING

SALT WATER   FRESH WATER

LIFE CYCLE OF THE ATLANTIC SALMON

NTIC SALMON
Salmo salar

Illustrated and designed by Michael Fraser Associates Ltd,
Inverness, Scotland

ISF/25/1/88

SMOLT

PARR

FRY

ALEVIN

OVA

These drawings are not to scale

Cock

Hen

'Kype'

Dramatic changes occur in salmon as they approach the spawning stage. Most noticeable is the 'kype' of the cockfish; a fearsome hook of cartilaginous tissue accommodated within a circular hole on the extended upper jaw. External changes in hen fish are mainly in colouration.

Predators

Throughout the life-cycle, salmon are preyed upon for food. In addition to those illustrated, predators include brown trout, eels, herons, otter, mink, porpoise and, of course, man.

Migration routes between spawning rivers and ocean feeding grounds.

6   Above and below: Two pictures of fishing from a boat with a
ghillie by Ernest Briggs, the eminent Victorian sporting artist.

8   *Gaffing the Salmon by Richard Ansdell.*

9   *The Lledr valley above Bettws y Coed in North Wales by Alfred de Breanski.*

10 *The Angler by William Orpren.*

11 *Coming to the Gaff by George Denholm Armour.*

The River Ewe, near Poolewe in Ross and Cromarty.

seem the same to him. The only variable which seems of importance lies in the shape and weight of the chosen fly. First it has to represent a small fish. I have shown in a previous book *Salmon Fishing* how the 'standard' single hook dressed in any normal pattern is transformed into a fish-like object when in the stream. I have also shown how a different type of fly, now known as the 'Waddington' presents a better image and fishes, especially in slacker water, at a better angle than the single hook. For those who are not familiar with the way in which the salmon fly evolved and with the reasons for the creation of this new type of fly I have extracted from *Salmon Fishing* a few paragraphs and illustrations and have placed them as an appendix (see page 179). That it is a benefit which the 'Waddington' fly confers, by being indubitably better at 'hooking' the taking fish, I am not now so sure. With the passing of the years I now watch with dismay the lengths to which some modern anglers will go, indeed I might even say, the depths to which they will descend, in their determination to kill a salmon. My sympathies now perhaps tend to lie with those who find that there is something not quite sporting in fishing treble hooks on a fly, and who believe that a single hook which gives the fish a better chance of getting off is the proper lure to fish with. I will certainly be told that this is an old-fashioned point of view.

Presenting the Fly

With what he knows about the salmon and the prey which the fish hunts during its ocean life, the thinking fisherman now must turn his attention towards the best method of presenting the simulation of this prey, his fly, to a possible taking fish. In other words he has to fish his fly in such a manner that it moves in the water at the right depth and, throughout the cast, at the speed at which a little fish can and does move. We have already proposed that the salmon lies in the deepest parts of the pool in the coldest part of the twenty-four hours. Furthermore, when feeding at sea in cold weather, it is accustomed to finding the shoals upon which it feeds lying in deep water. Salmon have been caught in nets set at no less than 300ft in the Northern Atlantic! So, in cold weather, in cold or cooling water the salmon would not expect to see its food other than in the deepest part of the pool. Anything swimming nearer to the surface would be unnatural and either of no interest or frightening.

Watching minnows swimming in a lake or off a pier in the sea, it is easy to see that they normally cruise around at not more than about 2 or 3mph. But, if alarmed, are capable of dashing off at three or four times this speed. This, too, would be the way in which small fish would move in the ocean. When fishing the speed at which the fly is moved must approximate to this.

We now arrive at the first of many problems. Standing on the bank, wading, or fishing from a boat we can cast our fly across the stream into calmer water on the far side. We can see such of our line as is just in the water gradually swinging over until it appears to be lying directly downstream below us. From the time it takes to do this we can estimate the speed at which the fly is moving. This speed is judged by us, land animals, as relative to the bank and to the bottom of the river. We see the fly as crossing the

The River Langa, a typical Iceland river yielding typically small fish.

stream quite slowly. But its true speed, as far as the salmon is concerned, is not relative to the bottom or to himself lying against a stone on the bottom, but to the speed of the current. If a fly is moving at say, 3mph relative to the bottom but is doing so in a stream flowing at 6mph, his true, or water speed is probably nearer to 8 or 9mph. The fish may not have much brain power but he is perfectly aware that if the fly is moving at this sort of speed it is something impossible and unnatural. The salmon will most certainly not take such a fly and may very well be scared away from taking for some time.

Consequently it is quite important that the fisherman, though he has no chance of seeing his fly in the water must study the flow of the current across the whole width of the river and must cast, more across or more downstream, as the speed and strength of the current dictates. The fly must, in principle, fish slowly with a water speed not exceeding that at which a little fish of the same size can swim. As already postulated in the previous chapter, the colder the water and the weather, the deeper should the fly be fished. In very cold conditions it is impossible to fish a fly, or a bait for that matter, as deeply as one would wish.

When the sun starts to raise the temperature, the salmon begins to look above the bottom layers of the river. In the sea it would expect to see the shoals of food fish beginning to rise as the day progressed. Your deeply fished fly is now behaving reasonably akin to these and, unless the day and the water both warm up considerably, will never have to be changed for something lighter to be fished nearer to the surface.

The finesse in fishing big fly with the sunk line lies in being aware of what it is doing. You cannot usually see more than a few feet of line before it disappears below the surface of the water. Only exceptionally can you see the fly itself in a clear river. As a general principle it is possible to judge the pace at which the fly is moving relative to the water speed by the pressure exerted on the line. This will be felt either by the fingers holding a spare loop or by the pull on the rod tip. It goes without saying that any excessive pull means that the fly is being whipped round across the stream far too fast. To ensure that this does not occur the fisherman must either cast far more downstream, far less squarely across the river, or must mend his line upstream immediately his fly hits the water, and often several times over.

Nevertheless the pull of the line which speeds up the fishing fly often creates a very realistic form of movement. You may imagine that a small fish, your fly, cruising gently around suddenly becomes aware of a large fish, the salmon, about to attack. What is its natural reaction? It is, of course, to dart away at full speed. So does your fly behave when being pulled out of slack water into the stream in which the salmon is lying. So, too, does it speed up when caught in eddies caused by big rocks and stones. This gives life and reality to the well-fished fly. But the moment it moves in a manner impossible for a fish of like size, the illusion is destroyed and the salmon frightened away. The ability to fish a deeply-sunk 8/0 fly at the proper speed and with sufficient life is probably the most difficult of all the skills. It is indeed a great art and is seldom understood even by experienced fishermen.

The advantage that the fly-fisherman has over his brother angler using the bait, lies in the fact that the latter, once he has cast his bait, ceases to have any control over how it fishes save in so far as he can speed up its progress by winding in faster. There is no way that the fisherman can slow down his bait by 'mending' and he is committed to fishing heavy sunken baits very fast, often too fast, in order to avoid getting snagged. It is difficult also to avoid winding the bait in too fast at the end of a cast since, if not wound in quickly enough when coming off the stream into slack water the bait too often sinks and is caught up in the shallows. But it is not easy with a bait fishing unseen in deep water, to judge when and how fast to start reeling in. The fly-fisher will know that it is here, when the fly comes off the stream into slacker water, that a high proportion of takes occur. He has no problem with his fly which he can fish carefully round until it is lying straight below him and can then gently handline it in before making the next cast.

69

Harling on the River Tay. No fish but a happy day.

The advantage that the bait often enjoys over the fly is demonstrated best in the big pools of big rivers. I recall when we fished Redgorton and the Stanley beats of the Tay in February and early March it was virtually impossible to cover more than a very small part of any pool with the fly as the water was too big to attempt wading. We always used to fly-fish the little areas we could reach from the bank and then revert to spinning. The great advantage that the bait enjoyed was that, cast square across the river, indeed even somewhat upstream, it could be allowed to sink naturally while being carried downstream with the current before being dragged across it by the line. Though the bank speed of the spinner in a strong current might be as much as 10mph, its water speed was no more than that required for the line to take it slowly across the pool. To a salmon the bait going downstream at 10mph in a current of that speed would appear perfectly normal. We used to fish the same pools out of the boat, not as you might imagine, casting as we did in early spring in the Gordon Castle beats of the Spey, but harling in a very specialized manner. The boat would be taken up to the top of the pool on its outboard engine and, with the engine running all the time, we would let out about 30ft of line. The boat would now be driven back and forth slowly across the stream and, at the same time, allowed to drift a few yards downstream at each crossing. That the engine and propeller were kept going all the time in no way prevented the fish taking. The ghillies were quite sure that the engines never scared the fish but rather woke them up. I found the same thing when I had the Garry fishings. The old Duke of Portland and the previous tenant used to troll Loch Oich with two boatmen rowing. I decided, against all local advice, to fish without any boatmen but with an outboard motor. To the amazement of all my motorised boat caught many more fish than our second boat which was rowed in the old way. Nowadays, of course, no one would dream of not using a motor for harling if they possessed one!

Bait fishing poses certain problems not faced by the fly-fisherman. I am, for instance, always astonished at the enormous steel case containing fold-back tiers of shelves and boxes which seem necessary for the 'complete' bait fisherman. Apart from a vast number of wooden and metal or plastic minnows of every size there is an assortment of spoons, of 'wobblers', of diving baits and sinking baits, self coloured and multicoloured baits and baits painted with luminescent dyes. All these together with a few snap tackles festooned with hooks for holding natural sand-eels and minnows and the inevitable spinners which impale cooked prawns comprise, with a selection of weights and anti-kink leads, the normal outfit which is complementary to a bait rod. As like as not there will be another container, box or bag also, which houses a number of reels. Faced with all this choice of tackle, how does the thinking fisherman make his selection for the start of the day?

Having put up his rod and having attached a multiplying reel fitted with a silk plaited line he must now decide what bait, from his vast collection, he will put on. The river, the Tay, is running clear and at winter level. On this sunny morning he knows that the flashing of a 4in Norwegian spoon fished rather fast across the lies can often prove irresistible. Perhaps a 3in Devon fished more slowly and more downstream would be more normal, or a large 'Mepp' fished even more slowly. Both these latter would need a fair amount of lead on the cast to get the bait down to the fish. On such a cold day, and so early in the year he does not have to think about spinning a prawn or fishing it 'sink and draw' as he might later on. Nor does he even consider fishing a worm as not only is it too early in the year, but the river is too high to fish this bait properly in the pools and not big and dirty enough to fish a bunch of worms in the backwaters. He decides on a Devon minnow of about 3in and rather fancies a 'Yellowbelly'. But being a thinking fisherman who has studied the probabilities of what the fish can be tempted with, he realizes that it really does not matter in the least what colour he chooses. He selects the 'Yellowbelly' because he thinks it looks rather attractive in the sunlight – as good a reason for the choice as any other!

The next problem is 'how much weight'? The answer to this will depend on how the angler intends to fish his bait. If he believes that he must cover as much water as possible with every cast he is committed to casting very square across the stream. He must also use a lot of lead to prevent the bait, which in any event is going to be dragged too fast across the stream, from feathering along the surface. This bait will fish reasonably for a few feet at the beginning, and for a few yards at the end of each throw. But this is obviously not the best way to fish a spinner down a pool. If, on the other hand, he prefers to fish his bait as slowly as is reasonable across the lies he will do so by casting more downstream and letting his bait sink naturally as it swings slowly across the river. He may not cover as much water in a big river but by fishing the bait slowly it will usually tempt many more fish than will a heavily weighted bait dragged too fast over all the lies.

Nevertheless there are, circumstances where the bait, cast very square, even slightly upstream, will catch fish which cannot be taken with more normal casting. In big pools such as those of the lower Tay many fish lie in very strong streams in some of the shallower pools of a very wide river. The only chance of catching such fish is by casting somewhat upstream. The bait now drops down naturally in the stream and does not start being dragged too fast until it has fished a lot of otherwise unfishable water.

A detail seldom considered but which may have no small effect upon the salmon's willingness to take or, more important, not to take, is the way the bait spins. In fast streams the standard Devon or other spinning bait rotates very fast and in so doing undoubtedly emits sound or shock waves which could be detected by the sensitive ears or nerves of the fish's median line in still water. The sounds of the fast moving stream probably mask these and it is unlikely that under such conditions the rate of spin of the bait makes any impression. Nevertheless experience tells me that in quiet water, a lake, for instance, the rate of spin of the bait can affect its efficiency in no small measure. When trolling in Loch Oich and the Garry river mouth in February we used dried or salted natural sprats or young herrings of anything from 4in to 6 or 7in, more or less as they happened to come handy, and of any colour, natural, blue or scarlet. These very large and unshapely baits were set on snap tackles with propeller-like wings at the head. With such clumsy rather flat sprats the wings were not very efficient at spinning the bait. But we very soon learnt that unless it rotated, even though slowly, the salmon would not look at them. Baits which lost a wing and ceased to rotate properly were seldom taken and, as a general rule, baits which were unbalanced or wobbled were not liked. Yet, move to the river, and we see that the most

The mouth of the River Garry. Colonel Ronnie Stanyforth fishing.

successful baits are those which spin fast or, like a Mepp, which vibrate fast. The movement of the water, as we have noted, probably masks the 'noise', and the eddies of the stream as it passes round or over rocks add realism and life to the spinner. The two most successful bait fishermen who I have known shared a further absolute requirement in the way their baits fished. They must lie level in the water. However weighted, the tail must not drop below the level of the head nor must the head be so weighted that it fishes below the level of the tail.

The problem of weighting the spinning bait in the early months of the year is one which has no easy solution. As we have already seen it is essential that the bait should fish as deeply as is practical while the river remains cold. But with the warming up of the water as the day progresses the depth at which it moves can, and probably should, be reduced. Beyond suggesting that, at the start of a February day, for instance, as much lead should be added to the cast as will allow the spinner to fish round as deeply as possible without getting snagged, little more can be said. Obviously whatever weight is suitable for the deeper and/or faster flowing streams will be too heavy when the bait moves into shallower and/or slower streams in the same pool. The fly-fisherman when fishing the floating line often likes to change his size of fly when moving from the fast flowing stream in the neck to the gentler flowing middle stretches, changing back again to the larger size as he fishes the swift flowing draw in the tail. I have no doubt but that the bait fisherman should ideally do the same; for if the bait and weight used is right for the faster streams then it cannot be correct for slacker water. If correct for deeper parts of the pool it cannot be right for the shallower reaches. It must also be remembered that, as everyone who has waded or swum down a good salmon pool over the favourite lies will know, the bottom has deeper holes very much favoured by resting fish. If such fish are interested only in 'food' which passes at approximately their own level and not in anything swimming above them, then these fish are virtually impossible to catch until circumstances in the shape of a warming river induce interest in prey passing nearer to the surface.

The thinking fisherman will realise that there is no way in which he can fish, either fly or bait, in the early weeks of the season so that whatever he arranges to do at the beginning of the day will be correct not only throughout the hours of the day but also throughout the length of the pools. He must therefore either be prepared to change the size, weight and way of fishing the fly or bait as the day progresses, or he must hope that with changes of light and temperature, with variations in the rate of flow and depth, the fly or bait chosen will prove correct for some part of the day and some parts of the pool. He will also know that because he has been successful with one bait

River Langa, Iceland. The sea pool and the tail of Crocodile pool at high tide. At low tide the fish cannot run into the river as the fall is too high to be jumped.

and one weight in one part of one pool at one moment of the day it does not signify that the same bait fished in the same manner will be any good at all at other times. The successful thinking fisherman will almost certainly be changing not only his fly or bait, but also the way he fishes it, many times during the day as he contemplates the changing conditions of temperature, light, and depth and flow of water in the pools of his beat. Though the floating line, small-fly fisherman of the summer will hotly deny it, catching salmon with the sunk line, big-fly or with bait in the early spring demands much more skill, knowledge and technique than any fishing later in the year. It is by far the most difficult of all the arts required in fishing.

The Change-Over Days

While the water and the air remain cold the problems confronting the thinking fisherman are, at least, straightforward. Because he understands the effects of slight rises and falls in temperature of a cold winter river on the behaviour of salmon, he can, on a typical early spring day, fish in a manner which has a reasonable chance of moving a fish. But the moment that the water temperature approaches a critical point, 48° F, the whole attitude and behaviour of the fish may change.

The salmon which maintains his own temperature at the same level as that of the water, behaves as if it were unconscious of the surface prior to achieving this. When 48° F is achieved and is maintained at or above this for a few days the fish can no longer be stirred by the big flies and baits of the early spring. Its interests now lie in much smaller lures fished quite close to the surface. Indeed it would seem that the salmon now sees its looked-for prey in reflection from the mirror beyond the cone of light through which it can see the outside world.

Once the river has warmed up permanently to 48° F or above, fishing becomes comparatively easy (though the confirmed floating line and tiny fly summer fisherman will hotly deny it!). There is a period though, often extending into several weeks, when the water temperature will rise during the day to above the magic figure only to fall at night to well below it. Also the height of the river can delay the change-over. At normal summer height the figure 48° F will be about right. With a rise in the water this figure will, apparently, rise to about 52° F. However, I am not sure but that this is an illusion. I believe the figure is as originally stated but that, in Scotland at any rate, much of the additional water will derive from melting snowfields and will reduce the temperature drastically at night.

This change-over period is probably the most difficult that the angler encounters throughout the season. It may last only a few days in fine warm weather, or several weeks in the frosty and cool weather so common in April and May in these islands. I recall one mid-May morning going to fish the Bridge Pool at Pitchroy on the Spey with my friend Captain Bill Johns (of 'Biggles' fame) who greeted me with the words 'We have been fishing all this fortnight without a fish. They don't seem to be looking at anything.' As the weather had been unusually cold for May I asked if they had tried big flies. He told me no, and that they only used greased-line in May. I suggested that someone should try big, early-spring flies and to prove my point put on a reel with a sinking line and a 8/0 Waddington fly. I came out of the pool with two fish first time down. Bill Johns then tried a big sunk fly and caught one fish and lost another. This proved too much for the ghillie Flockhart, who was not only sceptical but who, at first, quietly thought we had gone mad. Unwillingly, he too must try a big fly, and he too took a fish. Very soon word got around and all who preferred the fly were again fishing as if in winter. It was not until into June that year that the middle Spey fished properly with floating line and small flies.

The author fishing in the Balbain pool at Tulchan on the River Spey.

The other side of the story is well illustrated by an occasion on an April day when I had one of the best Tulchan beats, 'D' beat it was called then, for the month. Cold weather and snow water had prevented the early runs from filling the higher beats of the Spey and we were rather short of our expected number of fish. My friend, Alec Mitchell, a coal-owner from Canada, decided to concentrate on the greased-line and small flies rather than the sunk line and big flies which we were all using. The day turned out warm and sunny with a pleasant southerly breeze. The fish, too, felt that summer was coming. The only salmon taken that day on all the Tulchan water was the one Alec caught on his No 6 Jenny fished with a floating line.

The fact is, of course, that for a period ranging from a few days to, often, weeks, as many or as few fish can be caught with the greased-line fly as with the big sunk fly or bait. What is quite certain is that no bastard method will succeed. There is no half-way house between the two methods of fly-fishing. Occasionally after all attempts to move a fish with proper summer tackle have failed, a 3in fly is, in desperation, tied to a long cast on the floating line and proceeds to catch a fish. Such a fly, because of its weight will sink well below the surface and fish almost as if tied to a sunk line. Though I have not infrequently seen a salmon taken in this manner I have yet to see a fish taken on a small greased-line fly fished deep on a heavy sinking line. Doubtless this has happened and doubtless I shall be told so.

To the thinking fisherman the problems posed by the 'change-over' days may prove less difficult to solve than for those who, without serious thought, fish by some rule of thumb method. At this time of the year, late spring, early summer, the completely equipped angler carries two fly rods and, if he wishes, a bait rod as well. He will, on arrival, note the height of the river and the temperature of the water which he will see as being only just below 48° F at ten o'clock. And he will reason that as the nights in mid-April are still long, the water temperature for a large part of the twenty-four hours will be well below that required for success with the small fly. The fish will still be oriented to hunting in deep water. Our thinking fisherman will have no hesitation in setting up his sunk line tackle and, win or lose, will persevere with the big fly or spinning bait until lunchtime.

The temperature taken before starting his afternoon fishing shows a considerable rise. The day is warm and sunny and it is certain that the rise in water temperature will continue for a few hours yet. The fish, he now proposes, must be beginning to look towards the surface. Certainly any shoals of little fish he might have been hunting in the sea would have been rising near to the surface. The fish's own temperature too is rising as that of the river rises and it is becoming increasingly active in outlook. It is time to try the greased-line and No 6 fly.

Until sundown, when the water starts to cool off again, the best chance of catching a fish lies with the small fly fished perhaps rather more slowly than would be normal later in the season. If this method proves no good, it may pay to revert to the sunk fly. The salmon are still not oriented towards the surface and it may well require longer hours of higher temperatures to instill this habit in them. The one thing that the thinking fisherman does *not* do is fish with a fly of medium size and weight, say a 2/0 or 3/0 and hope that this imagined compromise will do the trick. There is, I must repeat and emphasize, no relationship between sunk and greased-line fishing. There is, too, no bastard method. Sunk and greased-line fishing are unrelated species which cannot be mated.

The angler may well wonder why this particular figure of 48° F should be so important. First he should remember that there is now no mystery as to where Atlantic salmon, with the exception of Baltic fish, go to feed. It goes where the gulf stream and the cold waters of the Arctic meet and where sea life, from plankton to whales, is most prolific. There is little doubt that for part of the year it is feeding fairly deep down on shoaling fish in the short days of mid-winter. Because the daylight is short and visibility not so good the salmon does not fare so well in this northern winter. The marking of his scales indicates a period of poor feeding. It may well be that the fish is driven to great depths to find food. It must be remembered too, that at temperatures approaching freezing, water behaves quite differently from any other liquid. The coldest water rises to the surface and turns to ice while the less cold sinks to the bottom. The fish, which has to endure this inversion of the normal is, nevertheless fully aware of it. In very cold conditions salmon in fresh water will inhabit the deepest pools they can find. Unlike the famous Punch cartoon clergyman surveying the advertisement for tube travel in midsummer who advocated, 'It's cooler down below', the salmon is not surprised. He knows that this is untrue. He knows that it's warmer down below. Better days arrive when the warm currents of the North Atlantic Drift, a branch of that mightiest of all rivers, the Gulf Stream, sweeps over the salmon's feeding grounds with the coming of summer. Now the shoals of small capelin, of copepods, shrimps, squid and young herring and the larvae of many species rise to the surface. The water temperature which induces this is, as the Mediterranean fishermen who then set their 'sardinal' at the surface know, about 50° F.

It is unsafe to generalize about when the 'change-over' days occur. Though I have seen fish taken in early March on a greased-line and No 6 fly – indeed I well remember when fishing Blackhall, watching Arthur Wood in the first week of March fishing with his single-handed rod taking a fish on a small fly from one of the jetties of his Carinton beat opposite me – one or two fish

*River Langa, Iceland. The tail of Kerstaffi pool where during the run
fresh fish go through every few seconds in a rising tide. They are usually
hooked in no more than 2ft of water.*

taken in this fashion as early as this are no more than the exceptions which
prove the rule. I have not the least doubt that such fish would be more
certainly caught if presented with the proper fly, fished in a normal manner.
More usually it is not until after the March equinox and its usual gales that
the angler need concern himself with the changes which the approach of
warmer weather and water bring.

Fortunately for the fisherman, these days and weeks of uncertainty
correspond in Britain with the arrival of some of the biggest runs of spring
and summer salmon. Such fish do not have the time which early winter runs
enjoy but are in much more of a hurry. They travel faster, and though resting
for appreciable periods, are 'on the move' in general terms, until they reach
one of the great holding pools of the middle and upper river. It is because of
this movement (you might almost call it a migration) that, while preparing
to run after resting and while preparing to rest after running, the salmon is
vulnerable. Once settled down to rest – to sleep? – he is no longer interested

Glentanar on the River Dee.

in hunting. While actually swimming upstream his mind is focused on finding his way and overcoming any obstacles. Only when he prepares to rest again does he become interested in hunting. Consequently, when large numbers of salmon are running up the river there is always a percentage of takers among them.

With the shoals of fish fresh in from the sea making their way towards the stretches of the river from which they can most easily reach their spawning areas, will run a number of the early fish which have been resident in the deeper, slower pools of the lower river. Nature ensures that, in the event of a prolonged spell of water so low that running is impossible, the bulk of the salmon destined to spawn in the upper reaches and tributaries will be near enough to take advantage of any little rise of water in the autumn to arrive at their destination.

Normally in March and April the river gradually drops away from full winter flow to summer levels. Now a steady proportion of these running fish continue to provide sport. Occasionally, however, if weather conditions are akin to being 'freak' they bring all hope of successful fishing to a standstill. Heavy frosts, often persisting throughout the daylight hours even into the month of May, can make angling a waste of time. Happily such conditions occur rarely and seldom last more than a day or two. Far worse, less uncommon and liable to last for weeks rather than days are prolonged spells of exceptionally low water. Low rainfall, cold nights and a shortage of

Evening fly-fishing on Durris on the River Dee. The boat is being lowered downstream on a coiled rope from an anchor.

snow on the hills can, in March and April make the river drop away to less than summer level in a few days. At such times not one fish can be caught by legitimate means. I recall one pre-war season when there was an enormous stock of fish in the Dee. I was fishing at Aboyne and had been down with some friends to the Potarch bridge where we were able to count over eight hundred salmon lying dormant in that part of the pool into which we could see. When I told this to my ghillie he said, 'Eight hundred – that's nothing. Wait till you see the Irrigation,' a pool on my beat the next day.

Sure enough the pool, when I went to fish it, was literally black with salmon lying head to tail and, apparently, two and three deep lying right down its whole length. 'They won't take and will look at nothing' said my ghillie, 'we've been trying everything for days. Never a move.'

I regret to have to confess that I did take out a couple of fish foul-hooked with a 3in fly and, to the surprise of all, another which actually took it genuinely. The ghillie, Lamont, whose name I shall always remember because of his very proper reaction to my deliberate attempts at foul-hooking with a fly, was disgusted and went home. Mortified, so did I.

Something that fishermen of today will find hard to credit is the fact that in those happy days of huge runs of spring fish, anglers expected that all the fish which they caught should look as if they had come out of the sea that day. The spring fishing was regarded as being over on the lower beats of such rivers as the Dee, the Tweed, the Tay and the Don by the last week of May, and even in the Spey, by mid-June. In the Dee, for instance, a few fished for grilse below Banchory until late June, but in the absence of an autumn run it would have been anathema to take and kill red salmon full of spawn. It will give the reader some idea of the change in attitude which prevails today from that of forty years ago when I relate that when forming a new batallion of Gordon Highlanders on Speyside in July 1940 the then tenant was unable to come up to Delfur and gave me the fishing.

Whenever possible I used to run down to the 'Two Stones' or the 'Back o' the Broom' in an afternoon or evening. It was, I realized later, a great year and I would catch anything from six to a dozen fish every day. Except for the odd fish which was absolutely fresh and which I could give to the Officers' or Sergeants' mess, I put everything back. They looked red to me and in those days 'gentlemen' did not kill red spawning fish.

How different today. No longer could anyone hope to catch anything like this number of fish day after day, and I feel fairly sure that no Spey fish caught in July would ever be put back!

I remember, too, when I had the lowest beat of Glentanar one year pre-war, I was standing and looking back over the Lorne pool which I had just fished unsuccessfully when my ghillie told me of his distress when:

Harling at Redgorton on the River Tay. A very overloaded boat.

'Some foreign sportsmen, continentals, I think' had taken some thirty fish out of the Lorne in the previous September and killed them. Today the beat is let in September at a rent which reflects the number of fish which are waiting to run the Tanar to spawn, and which are taken and killed in this month. I regret to have to say that this story illustrates what is the norm today and is virtually true of every erstwhile spring river.

Fishing from a boat is sometimes necessary on big rivers. Various ways of managing the boat are available and some are certainly better than others. On very big pools it is often necessary to lower the boat down the stream itself if the best of the lies are to be covered properly. Large sections of such rivers as the Shannon, the Wye, the lower Tay and even the Spey need the boat well out into the stream. Each locality has its own preferred method of managing the boat. The 'otter' method, wherein the boat is held by the ghillie from the bank on a rope attached to a pin on the nearside, works well as long as the boat does not have to be manoeuvred far from the bank. When I fished the Gordon Castle Braes beat of the Spey, the ghillie would put on waders and hold the boat while in the water. Holding the boat he could wade safely where it was difficult to do so without its support. In deeper pools on the lower Tay the ghillie sometimes uses oars, and many are remarkably adept at letting the boat slowly downstream while the angler casts from it. I have also known the boat at Redgorton to be managed in this fashion with an outboard engine, both for casting as well as for harling. For the single-handed fisherman who needs a boat, the simple way of anchoring with a long rope attached, and letting out the boat a yard or two at a time between casts is the best. With a ghillie on board as well the boat can be moved from one side of the stream to the other by his holding the rope from alternate sides of the boat.

There is, however, one serious disadvantage in fishing from a boat, which is too seldom considered or recognized. It is the same as that often encountered when casting from a bank or path higher than the water level, namely that whereas the fish probably cannot see the fisherman (and vice versa), they can see a 15 or 16ft rod being waved within their line of sight through the surface of the water. To illustrate this I have borrowed the diagram which Dr Mottram used when explaining the importance of this very point in fishing for trout. (*See* Appendix, page 173).

In little rivers such as the A'an, the main tributary of the Spey which runs gin-clear except in spates, the fisherman is usually very aware of the dangers of the fish seeing him or of it seeing anything which moves unnaturally. On this account we seldom used other than a small trout rod with the fly and, more often, fished a 1½in minnow cast from a tiny 4 or 5ft rod. The fish would certainly have seen and been frightened by any attempt to use a rod such as that with which we were fishing fly on the Spey. At all times when fishing any river off the bank the question of whether you can be seen, whether your rod can be seen, must be studied. The expert dry-fly trout fisherman on a chalk stream never goes near the river until he is sure that the fish he is going to try for cannot see either him or his rod. The salmon fisherman in small rivers or wherever he is fishing off high banks, must adopt the same attitude and precautions.

The Greased-Line and Small Fly

Once the water temperature has reached and passed the magical 48° F and has remained above this figure permanently everything changes. The fish now looks at the surface and, more particularly, at the mirror which surrounds the bright circle of light immediately above it and in which it can see a reflection of all that is moving around it. The fish no longer interests itself in flies or baits which simulate the small fish on which it feeds for part of the year in the ocean. Now, probably with the coming of the longer, warmer days of spring, the salmon in the sea experiences the astonishing transformation which the inflorescence of algae brings to those areas where warm and cold currents meet and intermingle. Not only do the salmon benefit from a new and overwhelmingly plentiful supply of food, but all the inhabitants up to and including the pelagic mammals feed and grow fat on the succession of living creatures which stem from this inflorescence. It is easy to understand why, with lengthening days, warming water and the springing to life of all that has lain dormant throughout the winter, the salmon in the river now remember the days, the weeks, perhaps the months, when food was plentiful and easy to catch – easier perhaps than the little fish which darted away when hunted – easy to see so near the surface and very, very nourishing.

I have said that there is no gradual transition for the angler from the big fly and bait of winter to the small greased-line fly and tiny baits of summer because I feel certain that there is no gradual evolution in the salmon's feeding habits or in the size of its prey. In the winter and early spring it is feeding on small fish at differing depths and in uncertain light – little fish which may not always be easy to find or easy to see. In the summer, in warmer water and longer and better light it is feeding on something very different – very plentiful, near the surface, easy to see and very easy to catch. If the whale can engulf millions of shrimps, thousands of prawns, hundreds of other arthropods and copepods, loligo and cephalopods by simply swimming along with an open mouth why should a salmon bother to hunt small fish? I do not think it does. I believe that the small fly fished with a floating or greased-line does not represent any fish. I believe it represents a shrimp or prawn or some other arthropod or cephalopod and I can see no reason why the krill which forms the basic food of many whales should not also be the basic food of the pelagic salmon during the spring and summer months. Small salmon flies are about the right size, are fished near the surface, and if not allowed to move too fast, can be fished in the eddies of a pool to simulate the movement of such a creature in the sea.

Having reflected on this the thinking fisherman who is going to try a fly is left in little doubt as to the right way to fish it. His fly represents a shrimp or a prawn. Both of these, when swimming, progress backwards and move through the water in jerks. Both have fine whiskers which trail behind them as they swim and all types are virtually colourless and semi-transparent in the water. The illusion that the fly must give is of such a creature.

The question of size of fly is the first thing which must be answered. Experience has shown that the basic size of greased-line fly is a No 6. This is the size which, in most salmon rivers running at normal summer heights, seems most readily taken in pools which may be termed standard. Any variation from this norm probably entails a change in the size of fly. For instance, should the river still be running rather high, and perhaps be a little coloured after a spate, a size 5, or even a 4 might be correct whereas, after a long spell with the water below summer level, flies as small as 10 and even 12 might be thought to be the only hope. In general, fast flowing rivers need bigger flies than do slower running rivers. For instance on the same day, under similar conditions, I will be fishing a No 6 in the Dee, while my friend is fishing a No 8 in the Don. In the Spey it may well be that at the same time a No 4 or 5 is the chosen size.

The thinking fisherman will ask himself why these variations should arise – indeed why is a No 6 size not correct for all conditions? Can it be that the salmon is aroused one day when the water is high only by a bigger fly which represents a bigger prey and when the water is low by a smaller fly recalling some much smaller prey? Can a fast flowing pool require a bigger fly than a slow pool because in the sea it is believed that bigger prey live in faster eddies of the ocean currents? In short, is the size of fly varied so that it represents a prey envisaged as differing in size when inhabiting different currents in the sea? I do not think so. Consider again what the salmon sees.

The late Fraser MacManus fishing the Ash pool at Kinnaird on the River Tay.

Ask yourself if a creature which has anything but the poorest of eyesight could possibly mistake such a monstrosity as a salmon fly for a fish? Remember, too, that the fly or bait which you are fishing with is seen through moving, swirling and very often somewhat dirty water. How then, you may well ask yourself, can this fish hope to differentiate between little fish of about an inch in length and others a quarter of an inch bigger or smaller and be prepared to attack the one but not the other?

For me the answer is clear. The small fly fished on the greased-line does not represent a fish. It represents one or other of the shrimps, prawns, arthropods or copepods on which the salmon undoubtedly feeds for much of the year and which give the salmon its distinctively coloured and energy-packed flesh. The angler fishes, not with a representation, but with an illusion. The small fly – it matters not whether it is of the 'bug' type, double-or single-hooked, the long shanked 'low water' or the Waddington type – could, with its hook in the tail of the fly, often with hackles streaming even beyond the hook, create the illusion to the wretched eyes of the salmon

89

of a much larger, but much more indistinct natural prey. The reason the only factor which can create or destroy the illusion is size, is that if the fly is too small for a big heavy running river, it will, when fished normally across the stream, be moving at a water speed too fast for anything of this size to attain. Unnatural movement is immediately noticeable even to a creature with very poor vision. I feel certain that many fish not only fail to take but are even put down by anglers fishing their flies or baits in an unnatural manner. Sometimes this is too slowly, more usually too fast.

If in low, clear water the fly is too big it ceases to be an illusion. Even the fish can see that it is a fly and not a shrimp. But with a too-big fly fish can often be caught if it can be fished in such a manner as to afford the salmon only a hurried sight of it. It often pays in low water to fish with say, a No 6 rather than move down to a No 8 or 10, but to fish it very fast over the lies. In shallow, fast running streams salmon will often snatch at a fly moving quickly past them even though they would disregard or move away from the same fly in slower flowing water.

What of colour? Does it matter? With the big sunk fly I have said that colour has no meaning for the fish which disregards colour and, though undoubtedly able to see and distinguish colour with its eye, fails to do so in its mind. It may be that the sunk fly, which is looked at against a background of the reflection of the bottom of the river, should preferably be of neutral tone rather than too bright or too dull. It represents a small fish swimming in the

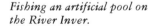

Fishing an artificial pool on the River Inver.

river. Experience has shown that the colour of the fly which represents such a fish has no effect on the willingness or otherwise of salmon to take it.

With the small fly, however, matters are perhaps somewhat different. Again we must consider that the fish is unreceptive and therefore unresponsive to colour. Now we are not presenting it with an imitation of its prey. We are presenting an illusion. Take three No 6 flies of any pattern, one a standard single hook, one a bug type so loved by Anthony Crossley on short double hooks, and one a Waddington type. Hold them in your hand and look at them. What on earth do they represent? If they are supposed to represent little fish why are they so small? Why, too, if they are little fish are they not in company with a number of bigger fish of their own species? And why, if indeed they are part of a shoal, should the salmon prefer to bother with these little ones rather than with the bigger mouthful of a bigger fish? No. It clearly will not do. The small fly definitely does not represent a fish, but it reminds the salmon of another type of plentiful food which it was accustomed to encounter near the surface of a warm sea. Again I have no doubt that this is a shrimp or prawn and that the reason these small flies – much smaller than most prawns – give the illusion necessary to arouse the salmon's interest is that shrimps and prawns swim backwards and are bent double at the end of each propelling stroke. The small fly, which is obviously solid in its core (the body) and may have feathers or little trebles trailing, gives, I believe, the illusion of a much bigger creature which is in part almost transparent in the water.

But, the thinking fisherman will ask himself, 'Why do I have to fish with smaller and smaller flies as the water level drops and the temperature rises?' I do not believe that changes in temperature affect the issue directly at all. Rising temperatures in the water automatically reduce the amount of dissolved oxygen available to the fish and there can be little doubt that for a start it causes it great discomfort, an accelerated rate of breathing, and may eventually lead to its death. Once the water temperature reaches about 65° F salmon in most rivers cease to take anything. They now face the problem of acquiring sufficient oxygen through their gills to keep themselves alive. Dropping river levels, however, mean reduced flow and, more important to the angler, much slower flow of the streams in which the fish are lying. In other words the fly fished in a normal manner will be passing much more slowly into and out of the fish's vision. If a No 6 fly is used the fish gets much too long and too clear a look at it. It now sees it is a salmon fly and not a shrimp. A much smaller fly cannot be seen so clearly and still creates the illusion. In many rivers in which the salmon lie habitually in water that appears to have virtually no flow at all, it becomes practically impossible to catch fish with the fly fished in the normal manner. In great stretches of

The Bridge pool at Balmoral on the River Dee. The ghillie, Brown, who was employed to look after the Crathie beat opposite was one of the most respected on the Dee.

holding pools in the Wye, for instance, you can catch salmon in the cold water of the late winter and spring with a 3in fly fished as if it were a bait. There is, however, no way that you can take a salmon on the small fly in one of these 'dead' pools. Sadly, fishing in many miles of this great river is confined to bait of one sort or another. In such rivers as the Thurso or the Brora many pools have to be fished by the angler, having cast his fly, walking backwards upstream. Very uncomfortable and deadly dull!

It may occasionally happen that the fisherman arrives on the river and finds that it has dropped several inches overnight. He sees that the flow is slower than on the previous day, but has little conception of how much even an inch drop in water level means to a fish. When, however, he wades into the neck of the pool, he realizes that even such a small drop in level means a great reduction in the volume of water and also in its speed of flow. He knows now that he should be fishing with a much smaller fly than the No 6 he was using yesterday – but he has no very small flies in his box. Nevertheless, because he realizes the reasons which create a demand for smaller flies in the changed circumstances of the day, he can adjust his method of fishing to compensate in some measure for his lack of these in his fly box. He knows that the illusion he must offer is like a conjuring trick. Show too much and the trick is exposed. Instead of reducing the size of the fly he uses too big an example but fishes it faster over the lies.

I wrote earlier that, compared with the techniques required to fish the big fly and sunk line well, those needed for the greased-line are simple and easy to learn and practise. I know that this statement will surprise many and may even cause resentment, especially in those who normally use a bait rod rather than the sunk 3in fly until they can fish the small fly. I should now, perhaps, amend this statement because there are two ways in which the small fly can be fished. There is the standard way universally used and adequately described in detail in every book on salmon fishing. Here we have a set of rules, easily learnt and easily practised. With a thermometer and a gauge giving the height of the water we can create a table giving the correct size of fly for all conditions likely to be encountered in the greased-line season. With a rough estimate of the brightness or otherwise of the day we can decide fairly accurately, if we consider it important, the colour and/or tone of the fly. And from a dozen or more written sources we can learn not to allow the fly to drag, how to fish rather square across the stream and mend the line, how not to strike at a rise. We can learn to change to a smaller size if we have a rise which does not touch the fly, or to a larger size if we are fishing a very strong stream in the neck of a pool. We can learn not to snatch the line off the water before the cast is fished out, not to allow the fly to float on the surface and not to allow the cast to become greasy and to float. We can

The River Tay near Pitlochry. A beautiful wading pool.

learn to fish the small fly with a cast of sufficient length. All this I say can be learnt from practically any book or magazine which deals with the subject. But there is another way of fishing the greased-line and the small fly which is not generally written about and which, for want of a better description, I shall call the 'expert' way.

Arthur Wood wrote, 'The basic size of the floating line fly is No 6'. There is no doubt at all about this. The No 6 is the basic size and it is up or down from this that all the practice of what I have designated standard floating line fishing derives. It is not only the size upon which the 'expert' way of fishing is based, but it is the size from which this method seldom allows change or variation.

If we accept that the art of floating line fishing is to present an illusion to the fish of what it imagines is its natural prey (even though it bears no resemblance to it), then to create this illusion in all sorts of different conditions with flies which are always fished in almost the same way, it is necessary to change, and to keep changing the fly, to meet the changing conditions. But if, instead of changing the size of the fly, we fish the fly we have nominated as the basic size in a different manner, can we arrive at the same conclusion? Can we create the same illusion in differing conditions and differing heights of water as we do (or believe we do!) by changing the size of fly? It is my contention that we can and that the best and most successful way of fishing the small fly is to do so in such a manner that however much river conditions change we need almost never change the size of the fly.

The thinking fisherman who has decided to be also an 'expert' goes down to the river and sets up his 15ft rod and floating line. He attaches a fine nylon cast of about 9ft which is carrying a No 6 fly. He picks the fly at random from his box. He believes the fish is indifferent to its colour. The first fly which comes to hand turns out to be a double-hooked Logie. Had it been a Blue Charm or a Silver Grey it would have been equally acceptable. He does not now wade in and start casting. First he takes a good look at the pool, its shape, how the stream runs in it, what sort of a run-out it has in the tail and what sort of a bottom. He notes, particularly, how fast the stream runs in the different areas between the neck and the tail and whether there are any backwaters alongside the main stream. For the thinking fisherman is going to fish his fly in each yard, each foot sometimes, differently from the next. The operative words are 'is going to fish his fly', and it is worth noting that they are not 'is going to let his fly fish'.

The Thinking Fisherman and the Small Fly

Ever since the 'Cairnton' method of fishing a small fly with a floating line was invented, a standard practice has been developed and has been written up by every author, in every book, in every magazine and periodical that has dealt with salmon fishing. Usually the advice refers to neat tables which correlate changes in the size of fly with changes in water temperature, with rises and falls in the height of the river and even, sometimes, with changes in barometric pressure. Tables, too, are popular giving colour and dressings of flies suitable for differing times of day, for bright and for cloudy weather, for clear and for dirty water and for the fast flowing necks of pools and for the comparatively dead water in the deeper parts of the same pools. These tables, if not learnt off by heart from constant reference, are kept handy for use at any moment throughout the day. In fact, they are designed to prevent the fisherman thinking about what he is doing, why he is doing it and about what he ought to be doing. They work perfectly well up to a point and, followed unthinkingly, will allow the angler to catch his share of the fish.

But to the thinking fisherman this is a very unsatisfactory way to set about catching salmon. Why, for instance, he asks himself, does the salmon prefer a No 6 fly when the water temperature is 48° F and a No 7 when it rises to 50° F? Why, when the water gets to over 60° F do we use ridiculous little flies like a No 10? When the water warms one or two degrees does the salmon feeding in the sea really pick out smaller fish from the shoal, smaller shrimps or prawns from the crowd of all sizes? The idea is illogical and absurd. Though rises in water temperature of even one or two degrees must affect the fish, whose own bodily temperature conforms to that of its surroundings, perhaps changes in bodily temperature may encourage or discourage the fish from taking. That such changes should allow the salmon to disregard a No 6 but attack a No 7 fly is endowing the fish with an intelligence and discrimination which it clearly does not possess, and allows it an acuity of vision which is denied by the structure of its eye.

Yet there is no doubt that, fished in the standard manner advised by every fishing book, the small fly, changed every so often to conform with changes in river temperatures, light, flow of water, etc. catches a fair number of fish. Fished in the same manner, flies which did not conform to what the 'Tables' demanded, might fail in the test of catching fish and we might therefore conclude that the best and only successful way to fish the small fly is that laid down in all the textbooks. I think that such a conclusion would be wrong.

Indeed, I go further. I think there is another way, a much better way, to fish the small fly. And it is a way which goes far towards explaining such curious anomalies as this one. Why, if I am fishing a good pool in the River Don and using a No 8 Blue Charm successfully, does my friend fishing a like pool in the Dee, only a few miles away, need a No 6 fly, and an angler wading one of the big fast pools of the lower Spey need a No 5 or even a No 4 on the same morning, when the air and water temperatures are the same in every case? By way of explanation you might conclude that the differences in fly sizes were caused by the fact that the Don flows throughout more slowly than the Dee which, in turn, does not compare for weight of water and speed of the stream with most of the Spey pools. Without realizing it, I think that in giving this explanation you would be well on the way to discovering a better and more successful way of fishing the small fly.

We must go back to basics. We have accepted that the small fly represents some small creature, copepod, loligo crustacean or the like, which inhabits the surface layers of the ocean during the long hours of daylight of a far northern summer. Here, where the diatom inflorescence in the mingling of the warm water of the Gulf Stream and the cold polar current gives rise to a food chain which has no parallel on earth, the salmon, together with many other ocean fish, and with mammals such as the seals and whales, graze and hunt and grow. It is perhaps worth noting that the most abundant creature among a host of crustacea, copepods and loligo which teem in the surface layers is the shrimp or prawn, a copepod which, known popularly as krill, forms the main summer food of the biggest creature which inhabits the earth, the blue whale. So abundant are the krill that, as every child who has ever been taught natural history knows, the whale simply opens his mouth as he swims slowly along, expels the water through special filters, and swallows the shrimps left inside. Since the now known feeding and growing grounds of most of the European Atlantic salmon are the same as those of the blue whale, it seems more than likely that krill, too, will be the basic summer food of the salmon. I would go further. I believe that not only does the behaviour of salmon in the river during the summer, and the choice of size of bait or fly that it can be persuaded to take, reflect the kind of food that has been its staple diet, but also the pinkness of the salmon's flesh makes it more sure that it derives from a diet of copepods. (Trout fishermen, especially those who have ever reared trout, will know that where there are no shrimps in the river or lake, the fish's flesh will be very white. Where there are shrimps and freshwater crayfish the trout will have nice pink flesh.)

So, the thinking fisherman, his rod set up, his floating line threaded through the rings and attached to a fine cast, now looks at his open fly box. The river is running at normal summer height on this fine May morning so he selects the standard fly – a No 6 – and the first that comes to hand is a Jenny. Had it been a Blue Charm or a Silver Grey it would have been equally acceptable. Colour has no meaning to the fish. He wades into the neck of the pool and starts fishing. At first he casts well downstream. His fly must not be dragged too fast across the lies by the narrow, heavy stream.

As he goes down the pool he starts to cast somewhat squarer and allows a pronounced belly to form and to drag the fly slightly over the main lies in the now less powerful stream. But when he arrives to fish that glassy glide in the tail of the pool which always holds fish and is always so difficult to fish successfully, he casts much more down stream and, with a quick mend of his line, tries to prevent any drag at all developing. Our thinking fisherman is fishing the standard salmon pool at normal height on a normal fine and fair May morning in a standard, normal way.

Though he would hotly deny it if accused of fishing in a purely automatic manner this, in fact, is exactly what he is doing. His knowledge and experience tells him that the fly he is using is the right size and that the colour and pattern is immaterial. He knows that he has to keep the fly moving, that he must avoid drag, and in the tail of the pool must be specially careful not to allow his fly to skate across the surface of the glide leaving a pronounced wake.

Fishing in this manner our friend will catch fish. He will, indeed, catch as many as the luckiest of his friends and a lot more than most. If the river drops a few inches he will simply change down to smaller flies and continue to fish the pool in exactly the same manner, casting at the same angles in the different areas of the pool, letting his smaller fly work its way across the now easier streams, and tending always to change the fly for a smaller one if he rises a fish which does not take. He will do so also if no fish has shown any interest throughout the length of the pool. In a falling river he will, too, be careful not to wade too deeply and will ensure that he is fishing a long

The River Shannon at Limerick.

enough line to prevent the fish being able to see the rod directly through the surface as it moves in casting. In springtime while there is still snow on the mountain tops he will know that the river will be falling at the start of the day, but will begin to rise later as some of the snow melts. He will, accordingly, having started the morning with a smaller fly, be prepared to try larger sizes in the afternoon.

When with overnight rain a small spate arrives, our fisherman will note that with a couple of inches more on the gauge the speed of the flow is disproportionately increased. With the water slightly coloured our friend feels it is necessary to try a fly somewhat larger than the standard. He attaches a No 5 and, because he thinks that perhaps it might be more easily seen than a darker fly, he chooses a bright yellow Garry Dog. He now fishes the pool down in exactly the same manner as he did the previous day in lower water. He casts the same length of line and at the same angles in the different parts of the pool. When, half way down, a good rise and a firm pull gives him a well-hooked fish, he is quite certain that he is fishing the right fly in the right way. Indeed, if it were suggested to him that there might be a better way of fishing this pool, he would be most unwilling to entertain the idea, let alone accept it. In a sense he would be right. Our fisherman has done

The Junction pool on the River Tweed. A great holding pool which also yields a lot of fish. But how deadly dull!

everything that a good, competent fly-fisher should do in the varying conditions he has encountered during his visits to this pool. And he has caught his fair share of fish.

When he goes home, as he packs up his rod and tackle he starts thinking. Could he have done better? Is there a better way of fishing the small fly when conditions of temperature, weather, light and water levels are all changing? He cannot reconcile himself to the apparent absurdity that a salmon should take a No 7 but refuse a No 6 in identical conditions, or would rise to a No 8 in a very warm river but disregard a No 7. Would this not indicate that the fish in the ocean picks out from many thousands of its natural prey only those which are of a certain and exact size and eschews all others? Also that if the ocean temperature rose or fell by a degree or two the salmon would feed only on a larger or a smaller member of the prey species? The idea is, to put it mildly, unattractive. There must be some other reason why the salmon is so definite in its choice of size of fly. Or, rather, why it appears to be so.

I have fished for over fifty years in the standard greased-line method first propounded by Mr Wood and elaborated or embellished with refinements by various practitioners and authors ever since. I, too, have made most convincing tables of size of fly changes to be made as water levels, temperature and weather altered during a summer's fishing. I have been through years of writing and believing that the colour and mixture of colours in the chosen fly was of prime importance. But it is only now that I have sold my guns and forsaken shooting that I have been able to devote all my thoughts to my first and greatest love, salmon fishing. The result has been that in the last few years I have come to believe that the standard way of fishing the greased-line small fly is out of date and basically all wrong. Why

Temperature	Size
48–50°	No. 4
50–52°	No. 5
52–54°	No. 6
54–56°	No. 7
56–58°	No. 8
58–60°	No. 9
60° and above	No. 10

Left and overleaf: *Typical tables for determining sizes of flies.*

Each size of fly is numbered in 'points', i.e. a No. 6 is worth 6 points. Therefore a water temperature of 52–54° is worth 6 points.

		Points
Temperature	53°	6
Speed of current	very fast	–2
Height of water	3in below normal	+1
Colour of water	clear	0
		—
		5
		—

A No. 5 is therefore the right size.

---

has no-one seriously thought to ask whether the method as practised originally at Cairnton and which has remained unchanged for over seventy years could be either varied or improved upon?

There is, however, a better and more successful way to fish, and it is a way which does not offend logical thinking and practice.

We must start with the fly. We have already decided that this represents to the fish a type of food which he finds in abundance during the spring and summer in the northern ocean in which he is feeding. For a number of reasons it seems most probable that this may be the crustacean which forms the staple diet of the Blue Whale, namely the krill. This small shrimp or prawn is no speedy swimmer but is content to move quietly along, browsing on the diatoms which surround it in their millions. But if alarmed, as anyone who can recall 'shrimping' with a net in their childhood will know, the marine crustaceans have the power of darting away, backwards in the case of shrimps, very fast for a short distance. If about to be attacked by a salmon there is no doubt that the crustacean does exactly this and the salmon will be accustomed to seeing his prey immediately propel itself away for a foot or two, pause while it straightens out in preparation for another dart, and repeat the performance until it is either caught or escapes. In other words the salmon, with very indifferent vision, is not too concerned with seeing if the fly looks anything like the shrimp which he is accustomed to catching, but will accept as a shrimp anything of about the same size and which moves like a shrimp under attack. That you, the angler, are concerned with making your fly appear in every detail as nearly as possible, in colour and shape, like that which you imagine the salmon's food looks, is a waste of time and effort.

102

River Vididalsa, Iceland. This river flows out of a north coast fjord and has much bigger fish (about 13lb average) than the Langa.

The fish itself is not interested in the detailed appearance of the fly. Provided it is of approximately the right size, as long as it moves in the way the fish expects, anything will do. A bigger fly will be expected to move faster, perhaps further too in each bound, than a smaller fly. If it moves steadily at a faster pace than a shrimp or prawn of like size could move, it ceases to be a morsel of food and becomes a frightening object to be avoided. If it moves too slowly, does not dart away from time to time when near the salmon, then it merely becomes another piece of flotsam floating down the stream.

The Thinking Fisherman (in capitals now!) is clear in his mind as to the method he should use when the season of the small fly and floating line arrives. He is going to fish his fly in such a manner that it moves in the same way as a shrimp or prawn, by 'leaps and bounds' perhaps, rather than in a steady progress across the pool.

The problem now arises, how is this to be achieved? Fortunately for the fisherman the natural flow of the river, over boulders and rocks which create little currents between and over them, imparts to the fly exactly this sort of 'life' and movement when fished in what I have described as the standard method of progressing down a pool. Experience has taught us all that a No 6 fly fished in this way in a river running at normal height on a normal early summer day will catch salmon. But change to a No 4 and fish the pool down in exactly the same manner and the fish will show no interest in it. A No 8, again fished down the same pool in the same manner, might perhaps produce a rise from a fish lying in the slack edge of the stream but would otherwise be ignored. Yet, let the river drop a couple of inches as it warms up and the No 6 will be ignored and the No 8 will produce results. Let it rain and raise the level a few inches and immediately the No 6 and No 8 can be discarded in favour of No 4 and No 5. How, you may ask yourself, can this be? Does the salmon really discriminate between creatures differing so little in size when conditions change slightly, and can it at the same time be fooled into thinking that a salmon fly is anything other than a salmon fly?

The answer, I find, is really very simple and straightforward. I cannot understand why neither I, nor anyone else, as far as I know, has seen it clearly before now. The salmon cannot see and is not interested in the detail of its prey. It is aware of its size and its eye is particularly sensitive to movement. In the environment in which it feeds voraciously, the ocean, anything which is of about the right size and moves in the right way is prey and is food. It does not have to examine it and it is not particular whether it is a bigger or a smaller specimen provided that, if big, it moves faster and further, if small more slowly and less far. If small and moving too fast for its size the fish cannot accept that this is an item of food. If big and not darting away quickly when near the predatory salmon the fish knows, too, that this is not one of its natural prey. In short, the salmon knows nothing about salmon flies, is totally uninterested in them, could not care less about their colour, their shape and, up to a point, their size. But it is interested in how they move. This, I believe, is the key to successful salmon fishing, not only with the fly but also with the bait.

When we talk about movement we refer not to anything positive, but to something which is relative to the observer. For instance, you may be sitting still in the train reading this. To your friend opposite you are motionless, but to an observer looking from a house alongside the railway you are moving at perhaps 100mph.

The salmon, resting by a rock in its chosen pool, has a somewhat different view of the movement and the speed of items in its surroundings. It has lived for all the months of its feeding and fast growing period in a medium in which there is no fixed reference point. In the open ocean it is impossible for the fish to know if it is living in a current or which way it is moving. In the river all has changed. The fish is now in a situation where it has a fixed

River Shin. Fishing from a platform below the Falls. A lot of fish hooked in this pool are not landed and the picture clearly shows why.

reference point – the river bottom. It is very well aware that everything in the water which is not drifting downstream at the river speed is a living creature. As he is virtually stationary on the bottom he is also very aware of the speed at which the river is flowing. Experience of catching and feeding on a variety of small prey throughout its sea life gives it an accurate assessment of the speeds at which, according to their size, they can move. It is upon this fact that the angler, fishing his fly, relies for success. It is the way in which the fly moves and its speed relative to the water speed, not speed relative to the observing salmon, that it is important. The smaller the fly, the slower must be its water speed. Conversely, the larger the fly, the faster must be its water speed.

For the salmon at ease in its chosen lie the main variable in its life is the height of the water. The river may fall steadily over a number of days, sometimes only of hours. It can rise feet in half a day in wet weather, or it can rise an inch or less every day when snow is melting slowly in the hills, only to fall back every night as the frost sets in. The importance of these rises and falls is not the effect it may, or may not, have on the fish, but on the speed of flow of the river. In winter and early spring when the river levels are high, small rises can pass practically unnoticed. But when summer levels prevail a small rise of an inch or two can double the amount and the speed of flow in the pools.

The Thinking Fisherman to whose notice these facts have been brought now realises the real reasons why, if fishing down a pool casting in the same manner at different heights, he has to change the size of fly to correlate with each change of flow. If he casts at, say, an angle of 45° with twenty yards of line out at all different heights of water his fly will move, as seen by the angler, slightly faster in higher water and slightly slower in lower water. The wading angler looks at the fly's speed from the point of view of an observer on the land. The fish, assessing the movement of the fly, will see its water speed as much faster in a higher river and much slower in a lower river. The salmon will judge the pace of the fly against the speed of the stream. The angler will judge it against the static bank or bottom on which he stands.

Here then is the real reason for the constant changes of fly. The lower river means a slower flow. Fished with the same casts as with a faster flowing stream the fisherman does not appreciably alter the speed at which his fly crosses the stream. But this fly, representing a shrimp, swims through the water too slowly for a real shrimp under attack from a salmon. The fisherman cannot alter the speed of the current, so to regain the illusion of reality he reduces the size of the fly. The smaller shrimp moves more slowly and less far at each dart. The smaller fly behaves like a smaller shrimp.

When the water rises the reverse takes place. The very small fly represents a shrimp that would be too small to swim fast enough even to maintain its position in much faster water. The salmon would spot this immediately and would be frightened by a fly moving with a water speed too fast for its size. The answer, so far, has always been to change the size of fly to suit the speed of the current. But, as I have pointed out, there is a better way.

A New Way with the Small Fly

The experienced angler will have acquired an ability to judge, from looking at a salmon pool, how deep the river flows, how the currents in the stream change, how the fly or bait behaves in different parts of the pool and how the pool will fish at different heights of water. He will, when he fishes it, also be able to judge whether his fly or bait is moving too fast or too slowly as it crosses the different areas of the pool, each having a differing water speed. This ability, often known as 'watermanship' cannot be taught but can only be acquired from experience. The observant angler who takes notice of every detail achieves good 'watermanship' more rapidly than his friend who is content to perfect his casting but merely allows his fly or bait to fish round mechanically.

'Watermanship' requires constant and detailed observation of water flow and speed, of effects of big boulders and rocks on the current, of little eddies and of sudden surges when the stream is forced through narrow gaps between rocks, of easing of the current as the pool deepens and of speeding up of the stream as it nears the glassy glide in the tail. The good 'waterman' observes every nuance in the flow of the stream and is aware of how his fly or bait is fishing through every foot of it. The good 'waterman' fishing down what might be described as a standard salmon pool (fast flowing neck with slowing flow in a deeper, wider central portion, leading to a shallowing and increasingly faster running tail) will, when fishing in the standard way, be prepared to change the size of his fly several times as he progresses down the pool. If wedded to theories which demand changes in colour and tone, or shape, he may also need to change as the sun comes out or as it starts to rain. In principle, he fishes with the same cast at the same angle the whole length

Pitchroy on the River Spey – a typical Spey pool.

of the pool but changes the size, shape and colour and perhaps the tone of the fly to suit as he believes, the different flow in different parts of his water. And when he gets it right he catches fish.

But, says the Thinking Fisherman to himself, why does he need to keep changing the size of his fly? This angler changes the colour and pattern because he believes the fish is sensitive to tone and colour: but the Thinking Fisherman disregards this. He is, as we have said, quite sure that neither has the least influence on the fish. But he changes size because the fly, as fished, is going to move at the same land speed but different water speeds in different parts of the pool. The natural swimming speed of what the salmon regards as its prey will vary in accordance with its size. The bigger the shrimp or little fish the faster it can swim, especially if chased or frightened. The salmon judges its speed, not in reference to itself nor to the bottom on which it is lying, but entirely in comparison with the speed of flow of the current in that part of the river in which its prey is swimming. In short, in the slacker parts of the stream a No 6, fished in what we have termed the

River Lochy. This is one of the only genuine late summer and autumn rivers which are not spate rivers.

standard way, and right for the faster flowing neck, moves with water speed which is unnaturally slow for this part. So the standard fisherman puts on a smaller fly whose natural water speed is correct for the smaller prey it represents.

So far we have been discussing fly-fishing. The bait fisherman, spinning a small minnow across the stream as he moves down the pool, solves the problem in a different manner. He does not usually think of changing the size of his bait; instead he casts downstream and winds in slowly in the fast running neck. In the slacker middle area he casts more squarely and winds in faster. If asked, he may well say that he fishes in this manner to prevent his bait getting hung up on the bottom. In fact, whether he knows it or not, he quite correctly fishes his bait like this because the water speeds with which it moves are correct for the different parts of the stream. I have often caught salmon in the gin-clear A'an casting straight upstream and reeling in as fast as possible to keep the little minnow spinning as it came straight downstream. Fish lying in quite hard water would sometimes turn, follow and seize it immediately. The land speed of the minnow might be well into double figures, but its water speed very low.

It must have occurred to many that if the bait can be fished successfully by varying the pace at which it is fished rather than varying its size, then the same method could be used by the flyfisher. For instance, rather than change to smaller sizes of fly as the river drops, why not continue with a No 6 but fish it faster. In a river swollen with rain, rather than put on a No 4 keep on the No 6 but cast much more downstream, mend often, and so fish the fly very slowly. I have now no doubt but that the best and most successful way of fishing the greased-line small fly is not to change the fly either as the pool is fished down, or as conditions of water and weather change during the day. Rather it is to choose, in general terms, the size of fly which appears to be best suited to the river height at the start of the day and, unless some very dramatic change in the river occurs, to continue with it. This means that the fisherman must learn to fish his fly through the pool. He must not merely cast it mechanically and allow it to drift round on its own. If he learns to do this well he will not only discover an added interest and pleasure in his sport, but will materially increase his chances of success.

The fisherman's first problem on reaching the river is one of determining what size of fly should be the right one for the day. Nothing can alter the fact, observed so many years ago with the birth of greased-line fishing, that a No 6 is the basic size. With the river running at normal spring height this is certainly the proper fly to use. This rule applies everywhere. In Norway, in that fastest of flowing rivers with its giant fish, the Aaro, we fished greased-line quite often, and quite successfully. No 6 was always the size of

River Carron. This pool, Louisa, is typical of a highland salmon river –
rocky, deep and relying on little spates for good fishing.

fly used. In the Brora or the Helmsdale when fishing pools which have to be 'backed up', it is a No 6 which is habitually picked as first choice. If the water is a few inches below summer level it would probably be easier to use a No 7 or even an 8, which would also possibly be the fly to try in drought conditions. In my opinion a No 8 is the smallest that should ever be used. Should the river be running a foot or more above summer level it might require less effort to fish with a No 5 rather than fishing a No 6 more slowly than is comfortable.

Let us suppose that we find the river at normal summer, late spring, height and that our chosen pool is one of my favourites, the Two Stones at Delfur on the Spey. This is a typical, standard, Spey pool. It is comparatively shallow, not more than 8 or 9ft deep anywhere with a good shingle bottom down which wading from the west bank is easy. The deepest water is under the high east bank and the pool, which lies mainly north and south, is slightly crescent shaped with northern tail tending to turn westward towards the next pool, the famous Back o' the Broom pool.

Our fisherman wades, not very far, into the head of the pool and starts to let out line. While compared with the much wider stream lower down, the rushing water in the neck is easily covered with quite a short cast. But in order that his No 6 fly shall cross the stream at a water speed suitable for its size the angler has to cast a much longer line, much more downstream, than would be necessary were he to fish a larger fly. He also has to make a series of mends to slow the fly down. He will be aware that in the heaviest stream the water is too fast for fish to be able to maintain themselves for long. He knows, however, that running fish will sometimes rest in the strongest streams for a short while, and that such fish are often willing takers. Not only do running fish like to rest in it, but a number which are temporarily resting may decide to take up more permanent residence in the rather easier flow at its edges. Unless our angler is careful the fly will come to a halt when it reaches the edge of the stream and lose the semblance of reality. Therefore, as soon as he feels the tension easing from his line the fisherman draws a foot or two in with his hand to keep the fly moving. It is quite surprising the number of fish which are hooked, usually rather badly hooked, when handlining in at the end of a cast. Most will be fish lying at the edge of the stream, but a few will be salmon that have followed the fly from the far side or the middle. The bait fisherman is very well aware of the importance of continuing to keep his spinner moving naturally when it has come off the stream. He, too, catches a fair proportion of his fish when continuing to reel in quietly at the end of his cast.

As our fisherman wades down, the pool gets wider and the stream slows down and deepens. As he looks at the oily swirls in the gently moving water he realises that this is greased-line water such as fishing dreams are made of. Every yard of this, the main part of the pool, looks as if it holds a fish – and indeed probably does! Now the fisherman has no problems. He casts a line long enough to cover most of the stream and mends occasionally when he feels that the tension on the line which he holds in his fingers is creating a drag on the fly. He watches the stream very carefully and, though he cannot see the fly itself, follows it in his imagination as it swings across, checking that it is not moving either too fast or too slowly. Finally he draws in a few feet of line before making another cast.

Where a large boulder or submerged rock causes a big eddy or a speeding up of the stream, special care in fishing the fly is needed. The fisherman may find it necessary to mend much of the line so that the fly hangs for a moment in quieter water before darting into the eddy and pulling quickly through it. I always remember the great lie in the Little Crooked, our best pool on the Invernesshire Garry, where four big rocks formed a sort of box. If there were any fish in the pool, there were always some which lay in this box. You could cast a fly from the jetty on the opposite bank into the box as often as you liked but you would never catch a fish. But cast slightly upstream and beyond

The Little Crooked pool on the River Garry. This wonderful pool fishes at all heights – even when the fish are forced into the rhododendrons in big spates. This river is always clear and is always in condition for fly-fishing.

the box, then the fly, dragged smartly over the fish by the pull of the line, more often than not proved irresistible. Those who did not know the river seldom caught fish in this pool off the right bank until someone showed them the trick.

Fortunately for our fisherman in the Spey, fishing his fly well requires no special techniques or tricks. With a light hold with his fingers on a small loop of line, with his rod held low so that any pull is felt directly by the fingers, the fisherman is in constant and direct touch with his fly. By varying the angle of his casting, by altering its length and by mending, he can control the way that the fly moves through the water. He can fish it rather than letting the fly fish itself. The experienced fisherman can feel when his fly is fishing too slowly or too fast. He can sense from the messages via his eyes and fingers when the fly is hanging in a slow running current or dragging through one of the fast running little currents which make up the overall flow of the stream.

We had a beautiful pool on the Invernesshire Garry called the Chest. To fish it there was a big rock on the right bank on which the angler stood and from which the whole pool could be reached quite easily. However, like many splendid looking pools in rocky rivers, there was only one lie and if there were a few fish in it they all congregated in this one small channel where the stream was forced between two big, flat rocks. The charm in fishing the Chest lay in the fact that you could always see the fish in the water and at the same time see your fly. Those who had never fished the river before could never catch fish in the Chest. They would cast perfectly across the lie and watch while the fly gently edged its way across the channel where the fish lay. Never a fish would stir. But if they could be persuaded to cast well upstream, to let a big belly form in the line and to drag the fly fast into and through the channel, it was nearly always successful. Fished in that manner the fly, to the angler on the bank, appeared to be moving far too fast. However, to the fish the same fly, now pulled by the tension on the line into swimming downstream, looked perfectly natural.

The occasions on which the fish and the fly or bait can both be seen while fishing a piece of water are very rare and it is, therefore, on the experience and the imagination of the angler that the ability to fish the fly properly and to best advantage must rest. Obviously, though the line floating quietly across the best of the pool may give the impression that the fly is fishing perfectly, there are so many little eddies, so many swirls, seen and unseen, so many 'mini-streams' where the water forces itself round and over rocks, that the fly will, in fact, be fishing perfectly in every cast for only part of its journey across the stream. For the rest of the time it will be travelling either too slowly or too fast.

Arthur Wood tells of casting square, even slightly upstream, and hooking fish on the far side of the stream in some of the Cairnton pools. Like many others I had never considered that this was other than a rather unsatisfactory way of fishing the far side of a stream which was almost out of reach with normal casting. Today, however, I can understand why this practice, properly carried out, can be very successful. The fly, cast in this manner immediately starts to float downstream but not as quickly as the line, which is being carried down much faster in the stronger midstream current. Unless a series of quick mends is made immediately, a belly is formed in the line which now begins to drag the fly partly across, but mostly directly, downstream. This dragged fly, to the fisherman, appears to be travelling much too fast. But to the fish it is merely swimming at the expected speed down a fast moving current.

Precisely the same happens with the bait. When I had the Redgorton beat of the Tay one February my friend and I used to get tired (and cold!) sitting harling in the boat in those enormous pools. So we used to fish quite often from the bank. This always required a very long cast to reach the best of the pool and our ghillie told us that the best results came from slightly upstream casts into the heart of the stream. This proved to be the case. Nearly all the

River Restigouche. This Canadian river is always fished from canoes. Here Mimi Ross has brought the fish into shallow water to be netted.

From left to right: Krill in sudden movement when alarmed; Krill at rest; Waddington flies (top to bottom Nos 8–5); Single-hooked flies (top to bottom Nos 8–5).

fish we caught took within a second or so of the bait landing in the water. We always regarded it as quite astonishing that we could catch fish like this, before the bait apparently had had a chance to start fishing properly. I now realise that the movement of the bait that proved so irresistible was when, having floated unchecked for a few feet, it was suddenly pulled sharply not only across but also downstream by the weight of water on the line.

Fishing the fly or bait properly means, in my opinion, discarding the well-worn and never updated methods of a generation which is now mostly gone. The more I study fishing techniques and methods the more certain I become that all ideas of colour being important, of minor details of size being anything other than a convenience for the angler, of tone being even noticed by the fish, are completely outdated. I am sure that the salmon in the longer hours of daylight and warmer waters of late spring and summer will have been feeding on shrimps or prawns (krill) as their basic food. Several fish netted at sea on their way to the Restigouche confirm this by their stomach contents. And I am sure that the small flies and baits which we use at these times of year do not represent small fish, but euphausids, which like, say, lobsters, crayfish, prawns and shrimps and their larvae, swim backwards

The Sand River in Norway which is famous for its big fish. The fisherman has gaffed the spinner, not the fish. He may easily lose the salmon.

118

by curling up their tails when attacked. In short, fishing the fly or bait properly, means nothing other than ensuring that it moves in as nearly similar a manner as possible to this type of prey which it represents.

The importance of the way in which the lure moves was never better illustrated to me than on a Sunday morning in one of those glorious pre-war years of huge runs of salmon. I was staying at Boughrood, on the Wye, when old Sir Harmood Harmood Banner suggested that one of the Johnston Houghtons, I forget which one, and I might care to fish that morning. His ghillie, Craven (I believe still alive) was told to take us down to the Home Catch, a big round, almost streamless pool, which we fished from a boat. Craven had fitted both of us out with spinning rods which he had baited with small prawns. My companion had, I think, fished very little previously. We moved, Craven at the oars, into the middle of the Home Catch and both started to cast from either end of the boat. To cut a not very long story short, there was a fresh run of fish newly entered into the pool and I think they were very tired. I very soon hooked one which swam, most obligingly, almost up to the boat. Instead of going ashore to land it, we gaffed it straight into the boat and went on fishing. Very soon I got another which again made no effort to fight and was gaffed into the boat. Before we stopped to go home for lunch I had caught six fish, all fresh-run, all so tired that not one of them took more than a minute or so to bring up to the boat, and we never had to land. But the astonishing thing was that my companion in the boat, though fishing the same bait, same lead, same everything, never had a touch. On one occasion I saw a fish following his bait almost to the boat when it suddenly turned on seeing my prawn approaching and took it. The reason? I think that he was probably fishing his bait too fast and that it was not moving in the way that a prawn in the sea would be expected to move. I was probably fishing at the correct speed from the 'salmon's eye' view. The other bait was perhaps moving too fast or too near the surface, too deep, too smoothly or too jerkily. We shall never know. There was nothing wrong with the bait, but only something in the way it was being fished.

Bait Fishing in Warm Water

Once the river warms up and the water temperature rises to 48° F and over, throughout the twenty-four hours, there is little doubt but that the fish are now sensitive to what is going on at and near the surface of the pool. Earlier in the year they have disregarded life or movement near the surface and have concentrated on movement in the deeper layers. Baits of three inches and upwards spun two or three feet below the surface will represent the small fish on which the salmon at sea probably lives in the cold, dark days of winter. The success of these baits in rivers running high and cold with melting snow is due to the fact that they can be weighted, they can be fished deep and can be fished as slowly as the angler wishes. The only problems which confront him concern the amount of lead that he should use and how fast he should fish his bait. The same problems confront the fly-fisher but are much more difficult to resolve. There is a limit to the size and weight of a fly which can be cast from even a 16ft rod. Often, I feel, the biggest and heaviest fly that can reasonably be cast, a 9/0, is not only too small but does not fish deep enough in really wintery conditions. The bait fisherman suffers from none of these restrictions and can fish really heavily leaded outsize baits as slowly or as fast as he likes.

When the time of greased-line fly-fishing arrives, however, bait fishing becomes much more difficult and, as a result, usually less effective than fishing with a small fly. Nevertheless it has its special place and use. But in bigger pools in sizeable rivers which afford good fly-fishing, casting a bait often becomes rather a waste of time and effort. For instance, the time taken winding in after every cast when fishing a bait down one of the big Spey pools is time lost. In little rivers such as the A'an, the main tributary of the

The Kattafoss pool on the River Langa in Iceland.

Spey, where fly-fishing is not always practical, spinning small baits can prove deadly. The reason that fly-fishing is not productive in many small rivers is that, unless only a small trout rod is used, the angler is always too near the lies where the fish are. As is the case with trout, nothing is more certain to put fish off than the sight of a fishing rod waving about over the pool. The dry-fly trout expert takes very good care to keep both himself and his rod out of the fish's sight. Many fishermen do not realize that salmon, too, are remarkably sensitive to any movement which takes place within their sight. I learnt a useful lesson in Iceland when we were tempted to look over the edge of a small cliff into one of the best pools of the Langa River to see if there were any fish. Unless we approached with the utmost care and scarcely showed the top of our heads over the edge the fish were, as our ghillie used to say, 'spooked'. They were then uncatchable for quite a while. It is for this reason that fishing a small river with a normal 15 or 16ft fly rod is virtually impossible. I always used to fish the A'an with a 10ft 6in trout rod. Even this was too big for many of the pools where only a very short line could be cast. Spinning or fishing any one of the different types of bait or spoon in summer water is successful only if extreme care is taken to see that the right size is chosen, and that it really spins properly and evenly. The spinner, Mepp, spoon, or any of a dozen minnow-type baits of every known

Tail of Kattarfoss in Iceland.

colour should also be fished at the water speed which a creature of like size could and would move in the presence of a voracious salmon.

The greatest all-round fisherman I have ever seen was the late Duncan MacNiven, proprietor of the Richmond Arms Hotel in Tomintoul, Upper Banffshire. He was the tenant of a mile or two of the bottom beats of the river A'an and I would estimate that he caught more fish himself in most seasons than any one rod fishing the best beats of the Spey. A very good fly caster, once the water warmed enough for the greased-line, he fished every foot of water in his pools which would fish with the fly, and he took a lot of fish. Early in the A'an's season (about the end of March when the first fish arrived) it was both uncomfortable and impracticable to fish the big fly on a sunk line in those clear streams fed with melting snow but if you wished to see a real genius at work you needed only to watch him fish a spinning bait early in the season or, later in the year, the upstream worm.

Duncan MacNiven was a perfectionist in fishing matters. With a four or five foot rod he could cast his bait to within a few inches of a rock or the opposite bank. His baits had to be perfect before he would use them. His favourite was a natural minnow which would, with a mouthlead inserted, be wired into a plastic, see-through scarab and have a double set of small treble hooks on nylon pushed through the mouthlead and attached to a swivel on

122

*Duncan McNiven, the greatest all-round salmon fisherman
I have ever seen.*

the cast. The scarab had always to be in perfect condition – no wings bent or broken – and the bait had to spin fast, evenly, and lie level while fishing.

For the first year or two that I had three miles of the best of the A'an I caught very few fish. Though very successful on my Spey beat, I had no idea as to how to fish this river. One day MacNiven passed by while I was trying to fish probably the best pool on the middle A'an, the Whirlpool. There were several fish in it but first with a fly, and afterwards with a bait such as I would use on the Spey, I failed to move anything. After watching me for a while, he said: 'You will never catch a salmon in this river if you fish like that. First you are fishing from the wrong side [though it looked to me to be the proper side] and second, no fish seeing your rod waving about over them is going to look at your bait. Also, it is far too big and does not spin properly.'

MacNiven fished with me for years afterwards and he taught me to fish this river with fly, bait and the upstream worm in the only manner that was really successful. I learnt, from watching him, how to set up my little 1½in to 2in natural minnows in their scarabs. How to make certain that any artificial baits such as 'Yellowbellies' (very popular at one time) or other wooden or metal minnows had both wings intact and that all baits, including Mepps, were fished at the right speed and at the right depth. He showed me how a bait cast slightly upstream and allowed to drift for a second or two without tension would often take a fish as it suddenly swung round when the

The Queen's pool on the River Dee from the Crathie bank with Balmoral in the background.

pull of the stream caught the line. MacNiven showed me how to catch fish by casting straight upstream and winding in as fast as possible as the minnow swam down the pool. I remember the first time that I saw a fish in my Balnedin Pool turn round, leave his lie and chase MacNiven's minnow straight downstream and take it within a foot or two of the bank where he was standing. I learnt more about salmon fishing from MacNiven than from all the years I had spent on some of the best beats of the best rivers in Scotland and, indeed, the world.

My friend Bill Johns, when he was tenant of Pitchroy and the fishing was a bit sticky, used to ask MacNiven down to show them how to catch a few fish. This he seldom failed to do and I remember very well one May day when the water was dead low and no-one had touched a fish for about a week, MacNiven turned up with his tiny rod and baby spinning baits and proceeded to take out a couple of fish first time down the Boat Pool. This gave all of us great hopes and we all tried spinning. But, alas, not only did we lack MacNiven's skill, but we did not have little baits which spun beautifully and fine lines and light tackle. We caught no more fish.

Captain W E Johns ('Biggles'), with the author at Pitchroy on the River Spey.

MacNiven's secret was really that he was a wonderful 'waterman'. He could look at a pool and could judge the pace and depth of the stream at every point. He knew exactly the right size of summer baits and exactly how fast and how deep to fish them. Above all he was meticulous in his attention to detail. He showed me, and dozens of others who stayed with him, that the secret of successful fishing with spinning baits in summertime lies in attention to every little detail. The speed at which these little baits should be fished is of paramount importance. I think it must always be remembered that almost certainly these baits do not represent a fish but rather a 'shrimp-like' prey. They should, therefore, move much more slowly than baits which represent fish. I think that this is the reason that so much care must be taken in the preparation of small spinning baits. If they spin well and fast they offer more resistance to the water and can be fished much more slowly without sinking too deeply. Mepps, for instance, can be fished quite near to the surface and very slowly, provided those of the right size can be fished properly. The small ones are usually too light to be cast easily.

When observing a well-stocked pool from a bridge, salmon will often be seen to move a foot or two towards a fly passing in front of them. It is very rare for them to follow the fly around. Those fish which take while handlining at the end of a cast are often described as 'having followed the fly out of the stream'. This is very seldom the case. These are almost always resting fish lying for a while at the edge of the stream. With the bait, however, things can be very different. I have often seen, in the clear waters of the A'an, fish following the bait right up to my feet. They never seem to take when they do this, though sometimes, when I am fishing out of a boat they will snatch at the bait when it is on the point of being lifted out of the water. I am driven, unwillingly, to the conclusion that in general small spinning or shimmering (i.e. Mepps, spoons) baits, properly constructed and skilfully fished, are more successful in the first place at attracting salmon. But once examined by the fish, perhaps at closer quarters, are not so realistic or inviting as the less flashy fly. Nevertheless the small summer spinning bait can, in small rivers where fly-fishing is impracticable, be a highly successful and attractive way of catching salmon.

The question of the right size of bait is sometimes difficult to determine. The problem is that, while for the most part, fishing at this time of year will be in rivers running at summer level, variations may occur and there will be a temptation to change the size of bait merely because the water has risen or fallen a few inches. Likewise, those wedded to the belief that colour is important may wish to change to different hued baits as the day or the water colour varies. This last poses no problem to those, like myself, who believe that colour does not exist for the salmon. The size of spinning bait which I would regard as the 'basic' in the summer is about a $1\frac{3}{4}$ minnow which should be fished with a water speed of about walking pace, or 3 to 4mph. If the river has risen and the streams are faster it may not be possible to fish this size of bait with a slow enough water speed. In this event it is necessary to increase the size to 2in or even $2\frac{1}{4}$in. The salmon is not going to be fooled by even the most attractive bait which moves faster than anything of its size could propel itself through the water. In like manner, if drought conditions prevail and the streams in the pools almost vanish, it would often pay to use a spinner of an inch or less. These, however, are usually impracticable to fish with and are too light to be cast. Fishing in these conditions with spinning or spoon-type baits is consequently nearly always a waste of time. There are however better ways of salmon fishing in dead low water than either fly-fishing or bait fishing.

Worm Fishing

For many of the older generation catching salmon with worms means one thing only. It refers to fishing a bunch of worms threaded on to a large single hook and fished only when a dirty spate renders all other forms of fishing useless. Under these conditions, when the river is too big and too dirty to allow fishing with even large Norwegian spoons, the last remaining hope for the angler is a bunch of worms. It is often quite astonishing how successful fishing in this manner can be. In much of the Spey, for instance, when the river comes down in a big spate the locals, by custom and long usage, appear to have the right to fish for sea trout in the evenings. (The Spey, incidentally, is almost certainly the best sea trout river in Britain with an average weight of a little over 3lb, but except in spates they are seldom fished for. Most are caught while fishing for salmon.) This fishing is almost always highly productive. In a big spate it is quite normal for one rod to take a dozen or so sea trout and a couple of salmon in an evening.

Fishing for salmon in a big, dirty river with a bunch of worms is exactly the same as for sea trout. It is usually easier to fish this quite heavy, but unleaded bunch, off a fly rod. The worms, cast underhand just far enough from the bank to reach the edge of the now roaring stream, are allowed to drift gently into the slacker water at the side. As the worms trundle their way downstream, line is let out and the worms are followed, often by walking after them, until something stops them. If it is a fish it will soon let the angler know by giving the bait one or two sharp tugs. Otherwise it is the bottom and the line must be reeled in and a fresh start upstream be made. Under these spate conditions little skill is required to catch fish. Nor is much luck needed. There is no question of having to find where the fish are lying. They are all congregated, a captive audience if you like, at the edge of the stream. In a well-stocked river this means a lot of fish in a small area.

The River Langa in Iceland.

Worm fishing of any sort is only successful when the water is warm enough for fishing the small fly on a floating line. It is a waste of time and effort attempting to fish the worm in even big, dirty spates unless the magic 48° F water temperature has been reached permanently. Evidently the pelagic worms themselves (of which there are many species) or the squid, cuttlefish or other loligo do not inhabit the same layers of the ocean as the salmon in the dark, cold days of winter. Until quite recently it would have been considered more than unsporting to fish the worm, except as a last resort in spates, in one of our great salmon rivers. Nowadays, however, it is quite common to see worm fishing in many of the best pools in some of our most famous salmon rivers when they are in perfect condition for fly or bait fishing. There are, for instance, several beats on the Wye where most of the fish caught during the season are taken on the worm. There are many anglers who fish nothing else and who, probably quite correctly, consider that their bag would be more than halved if worm fishing were outlawed.

To demonstrate how deadly a single worm fished skilfully in a well-stocked pool at normal heights can be, I will quote my experience of this in Iceland. When we took the River Langa, one of the terms of our lease was that on certain days one or two named local inhabitants could fish the Janni pool above the falls. This they did with a short, stiff rod, a heavy nylon line and cast and a single lugworm threaded on to a big hook. Their terms included the proviso that each rod was not allowed to take more than thirty fish in the day! And this number they nearly always achieved. There was no question of 'playing' the fish. As soon as it was felt that the salmon had a proper hold it was unceremoniously hauled straight out of the river and dropped, struggling, on to the bank. When fish are running freshly into a pool the worm is a very effective bait. (Incidentally, though the worm is always the bait chosen by the natives, there are no worms in the rocky lava of the Icelandic 'soil'. They are bred specially near Reykjavik and sold for fishing!)

In many rivers fishing for salmon with a worm is forbidden. It is considered unsporting to tempt fish with real food rather than with artificial flies and baits which it mistakes for food. This is a perfectly valid argument, and to many, like myself, reinforces the view that, in any event, if catching fish is your only requirement, fishing with rod and line is stupid. You should use a net. I feel very strongly that in high class salmon rivers, running at normal heights, fishing the worm in pools should be discouraged.

I am in no doubt about what the worm represents. The single worm unquestionably looks to the fish exactly what it is – a worm – of which dozens of species exist in both the upper and the lower strata of the sea and which would form an easily found and caught item of food. The bunch of

The author fishing Kattafoss pool.

worms might be seen in the unclear waters of a spate river as a small octopus or other cephalopod or loligo which, again, frequent the salmon's pelagic feeding grounds in large numbers.

It is not that fishing the worm harms the pool in any way. Indeed, carefully fished, the worm causes far less disturbance than either fly or bait. If the fish do not take the worm they willingly allow it to pass by them within inches without moving or taking the slightest notice. But when it is in the mood to take the worm, the salmon very evidently enjoys it as a tit-bit! The fish knows that this worm has little power of movement and cannot swim away, so there is no need to seize it viciously. He catches it quietly in his lips and proceeds to chew it gently. He then takes it fully into his mouth and begins to pass it into his throat. It is not, usually, until he feels the hooks beginning to prick him that he moves away from his lie with the worm.

I think that the objection to worm fishing lies in the fact that the whole ethos of salmon fishing rests on tempting a non-feeding creature into going through the motions of feeding by presenting the simulation of what is believed to be its food in the sea. The worm is not a simulation and, whereas no one ever saw a salmon which had swallowed a fly or a spinner, given time a salmon will certainly chew and pass a worm into its throat and gullet. In short, if the salmon is fool enough to take such monstrosities as salmon flies and spinning baits he deserves to be caught. The fisherman has fooled him, won the game and takes the prize. But catching him with a worm in a well-stocked pool is rather like catching a pike on a trimmer with live bait.

I am glad to say that in many of the best rivers fishing the worm at normal summer heights is rendered wellnigh impossible. Where there are trout these always seem to go for the worm before the salmon get a chance. Eels are even worse. When the smolts are moving downstream in their thousands they never leave a worm alone. Attempting to fish down a pool in such rivers becomes very tedious. It is annoying when the worm has to be replaced every minute or two. And happily, too, good salmon pools in bigger rivers have bottoms full of big rocks and boulders. Where worm fishing is attempted these soon become festooned with broken tackles and lines.

Upstream worm fishing in low warm water is quite another matter. In many small rivers which run very clear this becomes virtually the only method of fishing that has any chance of success at low summer levels and even lower. Of all the different ways of catching salmon legitimately this requires the most skill and knowledge.

The first requirement is the correct tackle. You can fish the upstream worm from a bait rod but not nearly as accurately as with a fly rod. The best is a somewhat stiff rod of about 11ft. The reel should carry a nylon monofil spinning line and the cast should be attached to it via a 'ball bearing' swivel.

This Bridge Run at Kylnadrochit on the River A'an holds surprising numbers of both salmon and sea trout. It fishes well with both fly and worm.

The cast should also be nylon monofil but of a lesser breaking strain than the line – for if one thing is certain it is that you are going to lose a lot of these casts in a day's fishing! The hooks are important. Some fishermen prefer to use large, about 9/0, single hooks and thread the worm on to them directly. These never look right to me and are not nearly as efficient in hooking as a Stewart Tackle of three small No 8 hooks or, better still, the same made up by the angler himself. It always surprises me how few fishermen are able to make up such a tackle with three-eyed hooks. It is almost impossible to describe the way of doing this in writing. But the skill needed can be learnt in a few minutes of demonstration.

Fishing a single worm always requires a little weight on the cast. In a low river the less weight the better The worm alone is not heavy enough to be cast any distance without some additional weight. To avoid, as far as possible, the bait getting snagged on the bottom is almost a priority, so it is essential to ensure that the weight is distributed evenly along the cast and not too near the bait. Even small spiral leads and split shot are too bulky and too easily caught up. Best by far is fine lead wire wound into a spiral around a long needle or piece of stiff wire which is then removed, leaving the spiral. Into this the nylon cast is wound. The lead is now screwed up tight on to the nylon. The end result is a weighted cast without protuberances to catch on the bottom. Worms can be bought and are usually perfectly satisfactory. But the best are those picked up with the aid of a torch at night from the lawn. If kept in moss (and fed if they are to be kept for long), they become quite tough and will stay on the hooks.

The well-prepared angler will have a flat tin containing a dozen or more casts which he has prepared the night before, hooked and weighted, and a small box attached to his belt into which he has put a little moss and two or three dozen good worms. With a pair of thigh waders he is now prepared to go into the river and start fishing.

Large salmon pools in big rivers are not usually worth attempting to fish with the worm except in very low water. Not only is the fly or the small bait generally more successful, but the annoyance caused by constant snagging if the worm is to be fished deeply enough, destroys all pleasure. However, salmon can easily be caught with the worm in most pools, especially in very low and warm water when they do not take anything else readily. The most satisfactory method is to cast underhand and rather upstream. The weighted worm should be allowed to sink and to swing round in the current in the same manner as a fly. When out of the current and in dead water, again the worm is carefully recovered very slowly in preparation for another cast. Often a fish will be felt to take as the worm is being pulled in, having followed round from out of the stream. Salmon often stop the worm as it

River Hrutafjardara – a fine stream under the cliff which may be full of fish one moment and empty of them a few minutes later. The fish run bigger than in most Iceland rivers.

passes beside their lies in the stream itself. The angler will see nothing and will feel nothing. He will merely be aware that his bait has come to a standstill. He now has to wait for several seconds – perhaps as long as a full half-minute – before it is safe to tighten up. Nine times out of ten it is the bait caught up on the bottom. Occasionally it is a small trout that has managed to swallow one of the hooks, or it is an eel, though these usually let go after a few nibbles. It is not a sea trout which always takes with a strong pull, leading to a quick dash away. The tenth time it may be a salmon. If so when the fisherman tightens up on him he begins, quite majestically as a rule, to move off.

Few anglers realize the number of salmon which, come low warm water in summer time, desert the pools and find a lie in comparatively shallow, fast running, rough areas between the pools. When wading these it is often surprising to find quite deep holes behind stones and rocks. It is in these holes that so many salmon – and, of course, sea trout – lie up and await a spate.

The skilful Thinking Fisherman realises that the bait he is using must not, like the fly or spinner, be 'fished'. A worm has practically no appreciable means of locomotion of its own so it must be allowed to be carried along by the different streams and eddies as it makes its way downstream. Cast underhand to a chosen spot slightly upstream of the angler, the worm is allowed to drift more or less along the bottom until it comes to a stop. Either a fish has stopped it or it is hung up. But while it continues downstream it must be allowed to go unchecked. The angler lets out more and more line while the bait is still moving.

A length of rough water is generally fished down in strips, the nearest being perhaps but a rod's length away from the angler; the next, perhaps, as far again, and so on until the whole width is covered. Likewise, the whole of a long rough can be covered by the angler himself moving downstream. Unlike the dry fly trout fisher, upstream worming for salmon requires the angler to move downstream. It is impracticable to wade the rough upstream in a salmon river.

Salmon usually take the upstream worm very gently in these shallow roughs. While sea trout often pull the bait hard and immediately run off with it, salmon tend merely to stop it. As in the pools, it may be several seconds before the angler feels the very light tug which the fish give on the line as they mouth the worm. Again, it is often impossible to determine for quite a while whether it is a salmon or a tiny trout which has stopped the bait.

Little more need be said about this fascinating form of salmon fishing. It is not a suitable way to fish everywhere. It is, used in good salmon pools in good rivers, a practice to be discouraged. But given the right small river, the right low water conditions and not many trout or eels about, then upstream worming can give sport of the highest quality. Some of my happiest fishing memories have been of warm, sunny summer afternoons wading in the roughs between pools in the A'an and of the epic fights which both salmon and sea trout put up when hooked in shallow water.

Fishing the Prawn

Summertime and the river running at normal heights with the water warm are the conditions best suited to prawn fishing. Indeed, when the water is still cold at the end of winter, salmon will not look at a prawn. When, too, the river starts to cool off with the longer nights of autumn, the prawn becomes a useless bait again.

There is something very mysterious about the prawn used as a bait for salmon. The normal way of presenting it in the mainland rivers of Britain is spinning. In Ireland it is often what is known as 'sink and draw'.

What does the spinning prawn represent to the salmon? The one thing of which I am quite certain is that it is not mistaken for a prawn. If you look at this monstrosity and reflect on the fact that it will be presented to the fish spinning backwards you must ask yourself what sort of an illusion you are creating? What does the salmon think that this is? I have no doubt at all what it is that this ridiculous looking bait is mistaken for by the salmon. That boiled prawns are red, or reddish, in colour has no significance at all to the fish. Dyed yellow or blue they work equally well, since colour, as I have emphasized often before, is unnoticed by it. The boiled prawn set up as a bait spinning backwards represents a form of food very common in the ocean. Loligo, cuttlefish, a form of octopus or cephalopod abound in the great feeding grounds of the ocean. When you look at the illustration of this swimming prawn and remember that its method of getting about is to propel itself head first, backwards, with its arms trailing behind it, you can understand how that ridiculous so-called imitation of a swimming prawn can look like something very different to the salmon.

As if to clinch the argument, the behaviour of salmon towards the spinning prawn reinforces the probability of the truth of this suggestion. Salmon are very prone to follow the prawn quite a long way before either

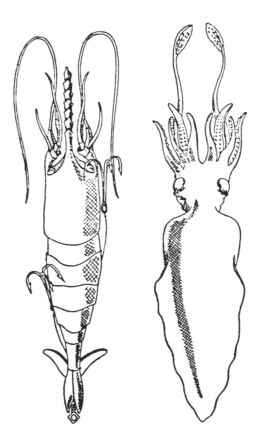

Prawn and Loligo

taking or refusing. I have already described a morning's fishing on the Wye when a number of fish could be seen from the stationary boat following the baits, and sometimes taking within a few feet of the boat itself. Not all these fish were takers or even potential takers. But they were all curious. Sometimes salmon, anyway some of them, seem determined to catch your spinning prawn and will come quite a long way to get it. At other times the prawn, the moment it touches the water, creates a situation which can only be described as panic. I remember once standing on the high bank on the Glentanar side of the Coble Pool (River Dee) when my opponent on the Dinnet side started to fish with a prawn. Pandemonium ensued. At first salmon started jumping out of the water in the stream where he started. Then I could see that wherever the prawn went fish immediately moved away to another lie further downstream and, in their haste to get away,

Below the paper mills on the River Don.

would often jump right out of the water. Eventually, as the prawn fished towards the tail, I could see fish dropping out of the pool itself.

What was the reason for this panic? Why do salmon sometimes take the prawn readily? Why are so many non-takers so interested? Why are salmon sometimes panic-stricken when a spinning prawn is fished down a pool? I think the answer is clear. The Latin name for the cuttlefish is *sepia*. The creature, when alarmed and chased, escapes by swimming backwards at the same time emitting a noxious black ink-like fluid. I do not doubt that the interest shown in, and the panic aroused by, this bait in salmon is owing to the fact that while the species *Sepia* are noxious, other loligo, possibly similar in appearance, are not. The one is good food, the other to be avoided at all costs.

Spinning prawns must not, in principle, be fished too near the surface. Because they form rather a bulky bait and are not heavy themselves they tend to fish very 'shallow', especially in fast streams. When allowed to fish too near the surface they tend to alarm the fish. I have noted that if fished fairly deep there is less likelihood of the prawn causing panic and a much better chance of it catching fish. It is essential to weight the cast enough to be sure of keeping the bait away from the surface of the water.

The proper way to fish a prawn so that it both looks like a prawn to the fish and behaves like the natural euphausid is to fish it 'sink and draw' in the Irish fashion. Here, with a good weight fastened to the cast, a foot to eighteen inches above the bait, the prawn is cast into the stream and allowed to sink. As soon as the weight hits the bottom it is pulled up a few inches and allowed to settle again further down stream. Meanwhile the prawn, usually on a single big hook, swings a few inches above the bottom at the end of the cast. This is a very effective method of fishing the prawn since the bait, always moving in 'fits and starts', gives a very lifelike representation.

Prawns for fishing purposes are always red and always boiled. Indeed I would hazard that this is the only way a lot of people, anglers included, have ever seen them. For the fisherman they are preserved in a number of different ways. Those bottled in formaldehyde are very messy to handle and tend to fall to pieces rather easily. Not to be recommended! Fresh prawns in brine suffer from being too delicate. Without doubt the best and easiest to handle are boiled prawns preserved in dry salt. Nowadays I see on my fishmonger's cold slab some beautiful, uncooked prawns preserved in salt. These are of an attractive green-grey colour and give the appearance of being slightly translucent. These are prawns in their natural state and, but for the fact that the salmon regards all colours as being colourless, these uncooked prawns would certainly have been discovered by now as successful baits.

Special Situations

The Thinking Fisherman is often faced with situations which require adjustment of his normal techniques. For instance his beat may include a bridge across the river. This, because the river is usually narrow where bridges are built, is often towards the head of a good salmon pool. Consequently much time is spent in looking at the fish lying in the pool and in trying to catch them off the bridge itself. It never fails to surprise the inexperienced how difficult it seems to be to catch one of the often hundreds of fish he can see lying in the pool directly below him. After spending valuable fishing minutes extending sometimes into hours, the angler, having tried every size and colour of fly or bait, eventually gives up trying to tempt those he can see. In desperation, he strips off yards of line and allows his fly, or bait, to drop downstream out of sight. It is now just as he starts walking off the bridge, reeling in, that the fish takes. It is not one of the fish he could see. It is one further down and out of his sight. More important, it is a fish which cannot see the angler!

The dry-fly trout fisherman is conscious at all times of the importance of keeping out of sight of the rising fish he is trying to catch. The salmon fisherman seldom bothers to give the matter a thought. This is often a grave error and, without doubt, is responsible for a number of lost opportunities and blank days.

Because this question of what the salmon is able and is unable to see is so important to successful fishing, I feel I do not need to apologise for repeating what must be 'old hat' to many thinking fishermen.

The laws of physics require that a fish lying on a rock five feet below the surface has a window through which he looks at the sky and the surroundings on the river banks and which extends to about 95°. Framing this window in prismatic colours is a frame of about 10° in which any features low down on the horizon can be barely distinguished. Beyond this no light from the river surface enters, and for the remaining 245° the light entering the fish's eye is from the bottom or the reflection of the bottom seen on the mirror-like underside of the surface. This means that the fish can only see clearly through a circle of about ten feet in diameter and increasingly darkly through rather less than a foot through the frame.

Further, all light which enters the water, except that from directly above the fish's eye, is bent by refraction downwards. The result is that any image which the fish sees near the edge of his window appears to the fish as if it were well up in the sky! (I should add that the fish, if seen lying in the water by the angler on the bank, appears much nearer the surface than it actually is. Anyone who has ever tried to shoot a pike in a trout stream will have found this out!)

What this means to the fisherman, in effect, is that if he, a 6ft man, is fishing for a salmon lying 5ft deep in the water, and wishes to keep out of sight of the fish, he must not approach nearer than 36ft from the edge of the salmon's 'window', i.e. a total of 41ft. At 40ft the top of the man's head will be visible to the fish. At 20ft he will be visible from the waist upwards, and at 5ft from the feet upwards.

Since in most fairly big salmon rivers all fly and bait fishing is practised with casts which are considerably in excess of 14 yards, the question of keeping out of sight when fishing off the bank does not arise until it is necessary to stand much above the water level. But there is one item which tends to be forgotten. The rod is likely to be about 15ft in length and, held at waist level, is effectively some 18ft long. To be sure that the 5ft-deep fish cannot see it waving about, casts of at least 37 yards have to be made. While cocktail bar fishing stories standardize 40-yard casts as the norm, it is my experience that not many fishermen are capable of making one, let alone fish a whole pool with fly-casts of this length. By wading, of course, the fisherman reduces the risk of being seen, man or rod, appreciably. The effective rod length is reduced to 15ft and the length of cast required to about 30 yards. Even this is longer than most fishermen care to cast and even for the young and expert is uncomfortable in any sort of wind.

Happily, things are not quite as bad as they seem. For one thing, light entering the edges of the fish's window is so reduced in intensity (most being reflected back off the surface) that until the moving rod tip can be seen through the clear window itself it may well pass, if not unnoticed, at least not as threatening danger. Also, in salmon fly-fishing, unlike dry-fly trout fishing where false casts are constantly made, there is often more than a minute required between casts while the fly fishes round. The salmon seems able to accept the minor disturbance of the sight of the tip of a fly-rod moving at such intervals among the rather hazy view of the surrounding bushes and trees on the river bank.

Salmon, too, very quickly accustom themselves to changes seen on the river bank. When fishing the Chest Pool in the Garry from a big rock (as already described in chapter 14) the angler, as he climbed and stood up, was in full view of the fish in their deep lie. Let him wait standing there and, within a minute or two, he has become part of the landscape. Provided no exaggerated movements were made he could cast quite normally without disturbing the fish. The background against which he was observed comprised tall trees and bushes which also moved in the wind.

A more remarkable example of how quickly salmon accept a new feature was always seen when we used to fish that wonderful little 'Whirlpool' on the Strathavon beat of the River A'an.

This pool could be fished at any height and, if there were any fish in the whole river, it was certain that there would be salmon in the 'Whirlpool'. It could be fished at summer levels with a fly, or at any height with a small spinning bait. The main lies were in the quite shallow water in the neck of the pool, a less frequented lie in the stream which was very shallow and which ran parallel to the main road, and after a further turn into the main lie, in a gully about 7ft deep, which ran almost under the right bank. This

A general view of the Whirlpool on the River A'an.

bank was about 15ft high and had one or two birch trees growing on it and literally overhanging the river. Though the pool turned left-handed throughout its 30 yards, and the observer would certainly think that it would fish best off the left bank, it could only be fished successfully off the high right bank with the deeper water on the same side. Throughout the early part of the season we used spinners or fly, but from about the middle of June onwards, when the spring run fish were becoming a little sophisticated and the river was warm and low, this was ideal water for upstream worming.

The neck and shallow stream were perfectly straightforward and were fished in the normal way. When the main lie was reached though, the angler had to climb on to the road and then make his way down to a rock jutting out from the bank under a birch tree. From this rock he looked straight down into the centre of the main lie immediately below him and not a foot out from the bank.

For a few minutes the fisherman would stand there. When he first arrived the salmon (there might be a dozen or more crowding into this lie) would quietly move away into the deeper water downstream or across into the shallows on the far side. But within five minutes they were all back again. By now the angler had become part of the scenery and the background. Very quietly his 10ft rod would be held over the stream. At first the fish would show a little unease over the slight movement needed for the rod, directly overhead, to drop the worm into the water. Very quickly they accepted this,

A close up of part of the Whirlpool showing the author standing over the lie fishing a worm.

143

too, as part of the scenery. When it moved it was doing little more than copying the movements of the branches of the overhanging birch tree.

Casting was nothing other than swinging the single worm, virtually unweighted, upstream and dropping it two or three yards above where the fish were lying. As the worm sank and was carried down into the lie the fish could be seen to turn, several at a time, to have a look at it. Occasionally one of them nudged it as it passed by. Then through the gin-clear water a fish could be seen to take the worm into its mouth and begin to chew it. For a start it did not move away with it but, perhaps when pricked by one of the hooks, began, after a minute or so to move. Still the fisherman does nothing. After what seems like an age the fish suddenly increases its pace of movement and gives a good pull on the line. It is probably now aware that something is wrong and is trying to rid itself of the worm, perhaps passing it out through its gills. Not until now does the fisherman tighten up and come to terms with his fish. All the while he has been watching with his polarized glasses every movement of bait and fish in the stream.

Some rivers have a number of pools which cannot be waded and have to be fished off a fairly high bank. Much of the Tamar is like this and I believe that the reason why these 'high banked' pools seem to be less productive than they should be is that the fish see too much of the rod and even of the angler himself. When the river is high, they do better – the banks are less high comparatively – but also, in a big water the Tamar is always dirty. The fish, consequently, can see less!

In very clear waters the problem of keeping out of sight is aggravated. In the little rivers like the A'an which we have been discussing it seems fairly obvious that care must be taken not to show too much to the fish. But in bigger rivers this is often forgotten. We had a wonderful looking pool on the Mid-Leisjne beat of the Laerdal which had a footpath running along an embankment on the deep side built to contain the river. We used to walk along this of an evening looking into the pool and trying to count the fish. It never occurred to us that the reason we never seemed to catch anything off this embankment until it was practically dark was that while we could see the fish they could see us and, because of the refraction, we would appear menacingly almost directly overhead.

We used to find it quite difficult to catch fish in a pool called Crocodile, the first after the sea pool, on the Langa in Iceland. This had to be fished off a bank two or three feet high. Most of the fish ran up under this bank, but the ones we caught generally came off the far side of the stream. I realise now that the fish under our bank could see far too much of us and our rods. In the next pool upstream we could wade and this kept us more out of sight. We caught many more fish here.

Contentment on the River Tweed at Kelso.

Some of the Langa pools lay under quite high cliffs and occasionally we would climb up to look at the fish. Our ghillie always tried to dissuade us from doing this. He said we would 'spook' the fish and would have to leave the pool for an hour or two before it would be worth fishing. Though we did not believe him at the time, he proved to be quite right. The moment our heads appeared over the edge of the cliff the fish would start to panic and move about all over the pool. It took them an hour and more to settle down again. I now realize that the eyes of salmon and trout are set in such a fashion that they have binocular vision over quite a wide angle (35 degrees) directly above and both in front of, and behind, their heads. Both as hunters and hunted (by seals etc.) they need this.

Fly-fishing for salmon from a boat is not always a success. It is very difficult to fish a two-handed rod properly when sitting down and almost certainly limits the angler to much shorter casts than he would otherwise use. This, of course, also allows the fish to see far too much of the rod in movement. While many people fish big rivers like the Shannon, the lower Spey or the Tweed with a fly while standing up in the boat, others find casting from this rather unsteady platform more than they can comfortably

Grilse fishing from a Shannon Cot on the River Shannon.

manage. I do not remember that we ever fished the lower Tay with a fly from a boat but always, if not simply harling, used a spinner.

Boats, incidentally, do not seem to have more than a very transient effect on salmon in either a river or a lake. A number of pools have boats used both for crossing and fishing. That these, crossing over the lies perhaps many times during the day, have any effect on the fish or their willingness to take, is impossible to detect. It always surprised me, for instance, that when trolling in quite shallow water with an engine and propeller running we could catch salmon with often no more than 15 yards of line out.

The most uncomfortable way of fishing from a boat is when it is being rowed by the ghillie or, worse, by two ghillies, who must prevent it from falling downstream too fast. Most uncomfortable of all is when the two, as in the Grimersta, converse together all the time in Gaelic. However skilful the rowers it never seems to the fisherman other than that the boat is either drifting down too fast, or is not moving at all.

Anchors, with a long rope which can be let out a yard or two at a time, make fishing in big, wide pools quite easy. These can be managed perfectly well by the fisherman himself, but with a ghillie the advantage gained is that, by holding the rope over one side or the other, the boat can be manoeuvered to either side of the stream as required. In some of the lower Spey beats the ghillie goes into the river in waders and holds the boat as he walks downstream. It has been known for the ghillie to stumble, let go of the boat and for the angler to find himself being carried through rapids before he could get out the oars.

When harling a pool in one of our big rivers it comforts many fishermen to realize that the bait always passes over the fish while the boat is still some 30ft or more upstream of it. Nevertheless, if the pool is fished out and the boat rowed back up the edge of the stream, and immediately harled down again, it may, indeed, prove more successful than first time down. Neither the boat nor the oars passing over the fish appear, as we have already noted, to have in any way upset them.

Even more surprising is the effect, or rather lack of effect, of a boat in a loch. When I first took over the River Garry fishings we used to fish Loch

Fly-fishing from a boat on the River Lochy. This needs a boatman who is very skilled to be successful.

147

Oich with my ghillies rowing the boats. In the old Duke of Portland's time two ghillies rowed each boat. The boats were rowed round the loch about 10 to 20 yards from the shore and the very big Garry fish used to take some monstrous 6 to 8in baits towed along some 30 to 40 feet behind. Neither the boat crossing over them nor the oars splashing upset the fish. Rather, these seemed to wake them up and perhaps induce them to take.

When my ghillie fell ill I was left to attempt fishing in the loch while rowing the boat myself. This would have been easy enough but for one thing. We always fished two rods out of the stern of the boat, one on either side. Whenever a fish took the first thing to be done was to stop the boat and turn it round. It always had to be turned to the same side as was the rod which took the fish. At the same time it was essential to reel in the second rod to prevent the hooked fish becoming tangled up with this line. Until this was done, no attempt was made to check the fish, which might be pulling off yards of line or, indeed, even to touch the other rod. With a ghillie and a fisherman in the boat this was easy. Single-handed, however, the temptation to take up the rod with the fish sometimes proved overwhelming. The resultant tangles all too often made it impossible to bring the fish in and it was lost. After much thought and many dire warnings, for the idea in those days of harling with a motor instead of rowers was considered outrageous, I decided to get myself an outboard and try fishing with it. It worked splendidly. Not only did the propeller not worry the fish but decidedly seemed to wake them up. Whereas my ghillie continued to row the other boat, my single-handed motorised boat produced nearly twice as many fish. Today I note that nearly all boats used on lochs for salmon fishing have outboard motors.

In common with the general practice we always ran the boat ashore to land our fish which the ghillie netted or gaffed. When fishing alone, however, this was not practicable so I used to move the boat into deeper water where there were no snags and net the fish directly into the boat. As a matter of fact, I found that this was very much easier than attempting to net them near the shore. The fish struggled far less in the final stages than when in shallow water. I now always recommend this to all my fellow anglers who fish from boats. Latterly we used to net directly into the boat most of the fish we hooked while harling in the Tay, though this was not quite as easy as when trolling in a loch!

Rivers, and there are many, which have big falls and 'falls pools' present certain problems. Falls which can be run fairly easily offer very little hindrance to the running fish. Usually the pool below such a fall fishes very well as long as the water remains cold. In summertime, with a warming river, such pools empty immediately. If the river drops too much such falls may become impassable and every fish seems bent on getting above them as quickly as possible.

There are a number of falls which can only be run in a big water. There are some, far fewer, which allow fish over only in dead low water. Such falls are those on the Sutherland Carron which, in most years, never drops throughout the summer to a level which allows the salmon to run them. If this river remains steady at normal summer levels the pool below the falls becomes so full of fish that they can be seen lying in serried ranks the one on top of the other, and fall easy prey to anything with a hook which 'sportsmen' drop in among them. If, however, the river drops to well below normal summer level, a number of the later run fish manage to struggle up this very difficult series of jumps into the twenty-five miles or so of perfect spawning areas of the upper river. There is a good case for banning all fishing in any falls pool where it is impossible not to foul-hook fish trapped by either high or low water.

Many falls have one or more fairly deep channels in the tail of the pools immediately above them. These form favourite lies for fish which have

River Laerdal, Norway. The 25-pounder has been taken on a spinner or spoon, but the smaller fish possibly caught on a greased-line with a single-handed trout rod – though I think probably on the spinning rod too.

jumped or run the falls. With their tails literally hanging over the edge these fish will often readily take a fly. If the falls are big there is little chance of landing the fish if it is allowed to drop back. We had such a lie on the Langa in Iceland at the top of some falls which were, in steps, at least thirty feet high. Many gave up fishing this most productive spot simply because they could not prevent the fish apparently falling back down the falls and being lost. They had forgotten the basic rule of playing fish in tricky places. If given a little line and never pulled, a salmon, unless completely exhausted, will always swim upstream against the drag of a slack line. These Langa fish could almost always be successfully played and landed, provided they were allowed to swim upstream immediately they were hooked.

Fishing below falls which fish attempt to jump rather than swim up sometimes provides surprises. Where there is no falls pool below them but only a few deeper streams, such as we had in the Garry, fish which jumped and failed often hit the rock and virtually knocked themselves out. Such fish usually fell back nearly on the surface into one of these streams and could be seen lying there. Fished in the normal way with small greased-line flies such as we were using in the pools, these salmon showed no interest. When a big 2in fly was cast over them they very often took it at once. I have no explanation for this seemingly impossible behaviour! Those who have fished below the Linn of Dee at Braemar will have experienced the same phenomenon.

Difficult Situations

Every now and then the fisherman will be faced with a situation, or set a problem which is not covered by the practice of his normal fishing methods. Many pools, for instance, which lie on a curve in the river will have the deep water under the 'outside' bank. Where both banks are available to the angler it is usually better to fish these from the shallower, 'inside' bank which is often easily waded. But on many beats with only one bank such pools have to be fished from the deep water side and this presents certain difficulties.

In the early season when the river is running at winter heights, fish do not lie in the main fastest flowing and deepest part of the stream. They lie in the rather easier flow of the edges of the stream. The best of these lies is usually on the inside of the curve. Wading here the fly or bait comes very naturally over the fish as it swings out of the faster water into the shallows. No problems here. Fishing from the other bank, however, the best chance lies on the far side of the stream. Casting normally, the heavy current immediately creates a big belly on the line and drags the fly or bait too fast and at the wrong angle over the fish. With the big fly or the bait this can be partly avoided by casting a very long line well downstream and, with a fly rod, mending immediately. This is not difficult and is usually quite effective.

There still remains the problem of catching the fish which is lying in the less turbulent water close to the angler's own bank. In the river running very full this may well mean that the fish on this side are confined to a narrow strip of easier water almost under the bank. Both fly and bait arrive in this water at the end of the cast almost 'dead'. The bait fisherman is aware of this and winds in as soon as the pull of the stream lessens the tension. It is now, as he starts to move his bait forward, that the fish may take. It is more difficult for the fly-fisherman. He must carefully pull in a few feet of line by hand at the end of every cast and must be careful not to allow the fly to hang

The Rock pool at Tulchan on the River Spey. A perfect example of a Spey fly pool. The wading is good from the east bank but there is a hand-built battery on the deep water of the west bank.

motionless over the lies. The golden rule is always that it is the natural movement of bait or fly which attracts the attention of the salmon. Likewise unnatural movement, or lack of movement, may frighten off the taking fish.

There are, of course, dozens of pools not on curves where the stream runs under one bank. Exactly the same tactics should be employed in all of them.

When fishing the small fly at summer heights it is not always easy to get the fly to move properly over the fish lying on the far side of the stream. Obviously long casts well downstream with immediate mending, helps to fish the fly reasonably over these lies. Sometimes, however, there are good lies at the extreme limit of the angler's ability to cast. Such was the case with Arthur Wood at Cairnton who preferred to fish single-handed off little jetties rather than to wade. He then, describing some of the nuances of greased-line fishing, suggested that in cases where he could only just reach the lies, he would often cast square across, even sometimes upstream, and allow the fly to float downstream unchecked. He was able thus to hook a number of fish which he could not otherwise have taken.

This is not the ideal way of fishing the fly. Unfortunately these words of Arthur Wood's, describing a 'trick' used only in rare and extreme situations, has led many fishermen to cast habitually in this manner. Casting and fishing the fly normally will usually be far more likely to succeed. Wood's method was merely a way of getting the fly to fish over salmon which he could not reach with a one-handed rod without wading. He would have caught even more fish if he had waded, used a bigger rod and fished the pool normally. Nevertheless, that split second when the free-floating fly was pulled into the stream often proved deadly. It was the natural movement of a small creature which suddenly realized it was in danger of being attacked.

Until the river gets very low the only fish which lie in, or just off, the fast-flowing broken water of the stream at the neck of the pool are fish resting while travelling. Such fish, usually few in number, provide a surprising number of takers. Since there is almost nothing that the angler can do other than cast downstream and mend to keep his fly from moving across too quickly, these are probably the easiest of all salmon to catch. In contrast, salmon lying in the glassy tail at the other end of the pool are almost certainly the most difficult.

That many salmon are hooked in these glassy tails might suggest that a high proportion of the fish in the pool lie here. This is not the case. It is true that as the light fails in the evening many sea trout and not a few salmon fall back and lie here, probably for an hour or two when preparing to continue

The author fishing the Phonas beat of the Ballindalloch water on the River Spey.

running. During the day though, nearly all the salmon in these tails can be classed as resting while running. Consequently they are vulnerable to the lure of the angler. The difficulty in catching them lies in the fact that they can see too much, too easily.

When fishing the big sunk fly or spinning bait early in the season, these glassy tails can be treated like every other area of the pool. The lure itself moves down among the fish and is seen long before the line comes into view. Provided the line is cast well and does not create too much splash, there is no difficulty in fishing these tails. A bad cast and tearing the line off the surface to rectify it causes a commotion which easily scares the fish. I have found that even the most perfect 'Spey' casts are often suspect for exactly this reason. The line rolling down on to the surface may splash too much and can alarm the fish.

With the small summer fly much more care must be taken. The problem here lies not with the movement of the fly but with the line. First, the floating line lies on the surface of the water and, as such, bends the surface slightly around itself. Beyond the 'window' through which the fish sees, the mirror of the surface is distorted by the line and creates a far bigger disturbance than would the line itself. Secondly, the colour of the line may have some importance. Lines are made in every colour and blend of colour that can be imagined. Each has its own protagonist and the reasons given for choosing a particular colour are generally wrong. For instance, there is a distinct tendency towards the use of white fly-lines in recent years. The argument is that they will show up less against the sky when viewed by the fish. This, of course, is a nonsense. When viewed against the sky through the fish's 'window' they will appear black as would any other coloured line. When viewed against the surrounding surface they will appear white against whatever may be the colour of the bottom of the river. On the whole a green line is more likely to blend with the colour of the bottom of most rivers, though a brownish yellow line might show up less in some Scottish rocky rivers containing much gravel.

One of the main problems in fishing these glassy glides which form the tails of many pools is that all forms of mending are out. The disturbance caused by lifting the line off the water and dropping it down again when mending is unacceptable to the fish. It follows that, with mending out of order, to be able to fish the fly slowly enough in the now rapidly accelerating flow, it is often necessary to make very long casts, very much downstream. The disadvantage of this is that the fly moves too slowly across and too smoothly speed-wise for the correct illusion to be maintained in many gravel filled pools. Where big rocks lie in the tail the fly moves in and out of the little eddies caused by them in a way which the fish find most appealing. I

Fishing from a canoe on the River Restigouche.

would estimate that a higher proportion of the fish lying in such rocky tails are caught than in any other part of any pool. I always recall fishing Pool Arder on the Lower Pitchroy beat of the Spey which I had for a season. For many years this had been one of the highest yielding pools in the middle Spey but was now filled badly with gravel. The whole pool lay on a curve in front of our hut and was only fishable from this side. The far bank was a small cliff. It always looked like a top class pool and we fished it regularly every day throughout the season. But for one morning when a guest of mine went in at the neck and pulled out three fish, one after another, none of us ever touched a fish the whole season in the pool proper. Pool Arder had a wide, shallow tail with a number of big rocks in it. During the summer we could wade across in a number of places and, except in holes behind some of these rocks, the water was not above three or four feet deep. In the spring this tail did not have the appearance of being any sort of salmon pool, but when the water fell to summer heights we began to notice a fish or two rising here. We then started to fish it seriously and, as the season progressed, took more and more fish out. We eventually discovered that this shallow tail of Pool Arder was by a long way the best 'taking' pool on the beat.

When the tail is shallow, streamy and the water broken, catching fish is

Campbell's Run pool on the River Carron.

much easier than in the glassy glides. The Corner Pool on the Amat beat of the river Carron (Sutherland) is like this, as also is the Bridge Pool at Glencalvie. Both of these look like typical salmon holding pools with fast broken water in the neck, ideal holding lies in the middle and a tail of rapidly shallowing streamy water. You expect to catch fish in the neck and in the deeper stream in the middle. In the springtime this is probably the case. But as the summer wears on more and more fish seem to lie, probably only resting while running, in the shallow streams between the big rocks in the tail. Twice as many fish are taken at this time of year in the tail as in the neck and middle together.

Advanced Techniques
and Common Errors

In writing this book I have assumed that the fisherman who reads it will be knowledgeable and experienced in all the standard forms of salmon fishing and will not require any further instruction in matters ranging from 'how to cast' to 'landing the played out fish' and all that lies in between. Nevertheless, I am constrained to write about certain errors not uncommonly noted and some special techniques not universally practised which may have escaped the notice of even the most experienced of anglers.

Though a modern carbon rod is a beautiful implement to fish with, not all are properly fitted to suit the individuals who buy them. For example, anyone selecting a new tennis racquet carefully chooses one with a thinner or thicker handle to suit his grip. How many fishermen bother to have the handles of their rods made to suit their hands? Yet they will have to hold their rods for many more hours each day than the tennis player. Again, few fishermen bother about the rings fitted to the rod. The top ring apart, there is only one really satisfactory ring which is at once functional and at the same time not easily broken. This is a snake ring. Likewise there is really only one kind of end button on a rod which is really comfortable. Since in playing a fish this has often to be dug into the stomach or groin of the angler, it must be soft and not too small. Small metal ends are anathema.

Many fishermen spend all day, and often part of the summer night too, in their waders. Yet it never fails to astonish me that so few bother to see that these fit them properly. It is always worth paying the top price for the best waders. We used to think that felt soles were the most comfortable and the most 'non-slip' available. So they were until the river got low and weedy. Tread on a weed covered stone in felt soles and you are lost. Far better, all round, are rubber or leather soles fitted with carbon steel tackets. These, like the motor tyres used in icy conditions, hold on rock and on slimy stone.

A very common error especially among the young and more active salmon fishermen is wading too deeply into the pools. It is very tempting, having looked into the river from a bridge and, having seen fish lying all across the pool, to make sure that the fly or bait covers especially the deep water on the far side of the stream. But by wading in too far the angler often ruins his chances by letting his fly arrive 'dead' and lifeless over the fish lying in the shallower water on his own side of the stream. These are usually running fish which are resting in the less heavy stream in which the fisherman is now wading. Such fish number a high proportion of 'takers' among them. There are many rivers and pools in others where much better results would be achieved if chest waders were forbidden and only thigh waders sanctioned. There are, too, a number of smaller rivers, like the Kyles of Sutherland rivers, where virtually all wading is both unnecessary and, quite rightly, often forbidden.

All fly-fishermen from time to time make a bad cast. Unless it is very bad it is usually best to allow the river to straighten and to fish it out to the end. In a strong adverse wind the line and fly in a number of casts may be blown back into a heap. Again, unless this appears an impossible mess and the fly is obviously caught up, it is best to leave this alone and to fish it out. The odd cast which fails to straighten out satisfactorily can immediately be lifted off the water and made again. But to do this often (I have seen the water being beaten literally into foam) is a great mistake and causes so much disturbance that the possible taking fish is more frightened than being simply wakened.

Many anglers have acquired the habit of 'waggling' their rods when fishing the fly round. This is done expressly for the purpose of imparting 'life' to the fly. On the whole I fear that, with a long line out, it fails in this since the elasticity in the line reduces the imparted movement so much that it is completely masked by that given naturally by the eddies in the stream. In a number of places, especially in the smooth, fast-running tails of many pools, any movement which disturbs the natural smooth swing of the line and cast causes an unnatural distraction which must at best, be disturbing, and at worst, definitely frightening to a fish. The major disadvantage of this practice, however, is apparent when a fish takes or rises intending to take. Now it is not always possible with either the big or the floating line fly to allow it to have slack immediately it is seen or felt. The movement of the rod tip may be pulling on the line at the instant when it should be allowing slack.

Bait fishermen sometimes appear to be in too much of a hurry. Many fail to fish the bait right round and then quietly reel in a few feet before rushing to regain their bait. Many cast and, before the bait has had time even to sink

The River Dee at Abergeldie.

and swing round, start to reel it in while still in the stream. This often commits the unforgiveable sin of dragging a spinning minnow along and across the surface. The art in spinning a bait lies in fishing it at the right depth, at the right speed and to the very end of each cast.

The length of the cast (now always nylon) used by fly-fishermen may have a profound effect upon the way the fly fishes and the success it has in interesting the salmon. With the sunk line and 3in fly there will not be very much difference, save in very slow streams, between a fly fished on a 3ft cast and on one of double that length. The line properly sinks nearly as well as the cast and fly, and in most cases, though by no means all, will fish at nearly the same depth with either length. With the small fly and with the line floating, the length of cast becomes of paramount importance. It is quite essential that the fish should be able to associate the small fly in the water with its reflection from the mirror of the under surface. In other words, the fly must in no circumstances be allowed to swim too deeply. It must, likewise, not be fished so near to the surface that its mirror image disappears or blends in with the reality. It would seem that the fish expects, or is accustomed to seeing the reflected image first, and that this alerts him to look for the reality. It is often tempting, especially in periods of low, clear water, to fish with exaggeratedly long, fine nylon casts. These would be fine if fishing American-style with a dry fly for salmon, but particularly in the now slacker streams of a low river these allow the fly to sink too deeply.

I cannot stress the importance of fishing all flies and baits at the right depth. When fly-fishing in the early season I do not believe that anglers give sufficient thought to the question of whether their flies are too heavy or too light, whether they are fishing too deeply or too near the surface for the temperature or the time of day, and whether their baits are too heavily weighted or are too light for the stream they are fishing. Bait fishing allows easy experiment by changing the amount of lead. With flies it is not so simple. I believe that, rather than have a box full of different patterns the fisherman would be better to have all flies of the same dressing but on shanks and hooks of different weights.

Much confusion exists as to the amount of pressure that can be put on a fish by a salmon rod. Held more or less upright it is quite surprising how little pressure can be exerted by even powerful salmon rods. It is not until the top and upper sections of the rod have bent into the state of pointing straight down the taut line that a little more pressure can be exerted by the lower, thicker section. Even so it is no more than a few pounds. If the fisherman goes into the water attached to the line he will be surprised that he can usually swim quite easily downstream against the pull of the rod. If, too, he cares to attach a cloth to the end and hold it in his mouth he will be horrified at the severe discomfort caused to teeth, jaws, and whole head and neck by the ratchet. I think there is a good case for insisting that salmon reels should all be fitted with an alternative form of braking or with a silent ratchet.

It is generally accepted that to land a hooked salmon it is necessary to tire him out. I doubt very much if this is indeed a true description of what happens. In the salmon we have, after all, a fish which is virtually a bundle of concentrated energy. It has built during its sea life sufficient stamina to allow it to swim many hundreds of miles, climb perhaps more than a thousand feet, create eggs or milt from a considerable proportion of its body, spawn and return to the sea and at the same time fast entirely for perhaps more than a year. How can such a creature be tired out by pulling for even many minutes against the pressure exerted by the rod? I think that 'tiring out' is an incorrect description of what happens. In order to utilize the energy stored in its muscles the salmon needs oxygen, and needs also to eliminate the carbon dioxide formed in this utilization. The only source of oxygen is that dissolved in the water which surrounds it. It is through the membranes of its gills that this exchange of gases occurs. The problem for the salmon, however, is that it has grown too big! In conformity with the unalterable laws of physics the gills of this fish increase their area in proportion to the square of the linear dimensions; his mass or weight, in proportion to the cube. In short, the trout can put up a much better struggle against the

12　The original Waddington flies which are now used all over the
world.

13　Examples of the new Waddington flies. Tied by Terry Ruane.

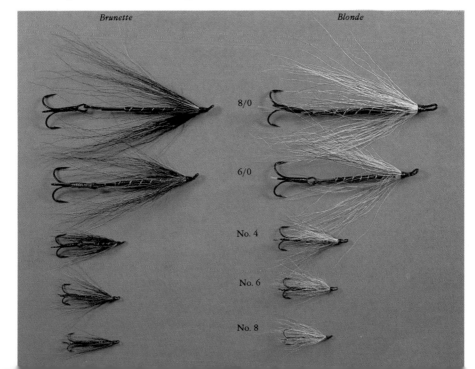

14 Netting a fish.

15 Fly fishing in the snow – usually quite successful.

16 *Corner Pool, Amat beat of the River Carron.*

17 *The River A'an – just above the junction with the Spey.*

18   Craig Lodge beat on the River Orchy. Early fish run straight
through the River Shin into the Orchy.

19   Fishing rough water in late spring.

20   *A fine brace of spring fish.*

21   *Salmon after spawning – note it has lost its teeth.*

22   *Fishing in the mist – he is probably wasting his time.*

23   *Wading on the lower Dee.*

24   *Falls pool on the River Forss – an easy leap for salmon.*

25   *1 Salmon, 2 Gilse or young salmon, 3 Salmon trout, 4 Great Lake trout – note the cannibal teeth, 5, 6 and 7 Lake trout, 8 River trout, 9 Parr.*

fisherman than can the salmon, ten times his weight but with only four times as much gill area.

The problem in landing very big fish lies not so much in that they pull harder or struggle more viciously. They do not. Indeed many seven pounders struggle far more vigorously than many fish five times their weight. The very big fish, because its gill area is too small for its weight, cannot breathe easily when under strain. It must rest and it is for this reason that big fish always seek the depths and find a stone or rock to lie behind, immobile. With the amount of pressure which it is possible to exert on them with the rod it is often quite impossible to move such fish and, in extreme cases, fishermen have allowed themselves to be holding on for over half a day. If, however, the monster can be kept moving it can be brought to the net (or gaff?) almost as quickly as a ten pounder. Beware of putting your key-ring round the line to slide down to the fish. If it then breaks away you may have lost the car key as well as those of the house!

One of the secrets of playing very big fish successfully is not to allow them, as would be normal, to keep level and swim across the stream into slacker water on the far side. If you allow very big salmon to get 'side on' into the stream the fish has merely to turn its head away from you when its body acts like an 'Otter'. The fish now uses no energy in pulling away from the rod. The current does all the work while the fish merely rests.

When I first went to fish the Aaro river I had not realized, when told that

River Aaro, Norway. Nicolai Denisoff ghillying for his guest, Sampson Field on one of the Aaro platforms.

it was a 'big fish' river, that the average weight of fish caught was about 30lbs and that any fish of under 25lbs was a rarity. The tenant at that time was a singular and most delightful Russian named Nicolai Denisoff. He had acquired the lease of this, perhaps with the Alta, the most sought after salmon river in the world, in the same manner that he had acquired great wealth in his youth. Trained as a singer he was a leading member of the Russian State Opera in Tsarist days. Nicolai, brought up a poor student, decided to become rich. He discovered that in pre-First World War days everything in Russia seemed to be run on a system of bribery. Very quickly he became the arch-briber. Before long he had not only become one of the richest men in Russia with a palace on the Black Sea bigger than the Tsar's but had so organized his affairs that he was able to leave at the time of the revolution with a fortune intact and with the sole agency for the distribution and sale of caviar. For many years after 1917 Nicolai Denisoff supported most of the Russian nobles etc. who had managed to escape to Paris virtually penniless.

The Aaro is a unique river. From the falls from the lake above to the top of the sea pool is less than a mile and of this at least half is an unfishable torrent. I think that the reason that the fish are so big is that no smaller salmon would have the strength to climb the rapids into any of the pools. Though several hundred sea trout used to be caught each season in the sea pool, none ever reached the 'salmon' stretches of this river. The fishable (salmon) part of the river is unwadeable and impossible for a boat. Until platforms were built, some extending right across the river, most attempts to fish the pools from the bank ended in failure. These big fish in powerful currents usually broke or forced the hooks out. Fishing the big fly from the platforms required a special technique. All the tackle, lines, casts and hooks, had to be virtually unbreakable. (We used always to test our thick gut casts and 9/0 hooks by putting the point of the hook into the wooden rail of the verandah and pulling as hard as possible. If anything could be broken something stronger must be used.) The technique required to land a fish hooked off one of these platforms was simple. If the fish were allowed to move sideways in the stream it would certainly either break something or pull the fly out of its hold. Playing the fish, then, became only a question of keeping directly above the fish and preventing it from turning sideways. This could only be achieved by pulling it as hard as possible. Surprisingly it was not difficult to prevent the fish from turning and, even more surprising, pulling it hard from directly above tired it more quickly than could have been expected with such big fish played in the normal way. I do not recall that any salmon took us more than about half an hour to edge sideways along the platform, a foot at a time, until we got him into the shallows and could gaff

More platforms on the River Aaro.

him. Indeed the fifty-plus pounder I caught was landed single-handed and tailed in less than forty minutes. The extraordinary thing about this fishing was the fact that these monster fish could be caught on a greased-line and a No 4 or No 5 fly. They too could be pulled very hard and landed using the same tactics.

When fishing with a boatman in a lake or in one of those great still pools such as are found on the Wye, it is usually better not to attempt to follow a fish as it runs but to keep the boat steady more or less in the same place. Nor is it necessary, even with the biggest fish, to go ashore to land it where there is little or no current. The oars can be safely shipped while the fish is netted into the boat. Where there is an outboard engine great care must be taken to see that a tiring fish does not run under the boat and foul the line between the keel and the engine. I have known many big fish lost in Loch Oich in this way. I once had a fish run round the mooring chain holding a buoy marking the channel of the Caledonian Canal in Loch Oich. The line was properly fouled up and eventually broke quite near the rod. The broken piece, however, remained attached to the chain and the fish to the line. For some time afterwards every now and then the buoy could be seen to nod sideways as the fish, a big Garry salmon, tried again to get away. I suppose it eventually got rid of the hooks as they always do.

Before the general use of outboard engines for trolling it used to be the fashion to use two boatmen to row and manoeuvre the boat. I never found this other than a somewhat tedious way of fishing. The boatmen conversed with each other and the angler was always made to feel the odd man out. When I went, a guest of one of the syndicate, to the Grimersta I spent my first two days catching about ten salmon each day. Since I was sitting casting a fly from a boat with two boatmen who spoke only the one to the other and only in Gaelic, I soon got tired of fishing like this. I telephoned my secretary to send me a telegram demanding urgent return home and left before my week was up. On another occasion I was fishing a famous beat, which shall be nameless, when I was given a pool which required a boat and two boatmen to manouevre it properly in a difficult stream. Absolute silence the length of the pool from the two men! Heaven for me! I discovered later that the one had seduced the wife of the other and, though both continued in the same employment, had not spoken a word to each other for years.

Autumn Fishing

Before embarking on catching salmon in the later months of the season the Thinking Fisherman should give some thought to the ethical question of whether it is either right or desirable to catch and kill breeding fish. As a general rule man protects breeding species by legislation which establishes a 'close' season, when killing members of the species is forbidden. This covers birds and animals quite successfully in most cases. Yet there are instances where the law allows, and custom encourages, the killing of breeding birds and mammals usually for sport. For instance the shooting of blackcock at the 'lek' or the courting capercaillie displaying, are considered prime springtime 'sports' by many of our continental neighbours. The stalking and shooting of roaring red deer stags from among the hinds in October is most certainly killing an animal in the breeding season but is a most sought after 'sport'. That the hinds are protected during the mating season but are then killed when pregnant in the new year seems a most astonishing aspect of a law designed to protect this species. Yet, on the whole, man's laws where animals are concerned achieve the purposes for which they were framed. There are, of course, many obvious anomalies.

The laws framed to protect salmon are, however, quite inexplicable. From ancient times close seasons for these fish were established in the sense that it was illegal to take any fish during the close period. But there is not, and never has been, any agreement between those responsible for each river as to what exactly should constitute the close season. The Aberdeenshire Dee for example used, historically, to close at the end of October and reopen on 11 February. During my lifetime these dates have been changed in stages to 15 September and 1 February while the Don, flowing out into the sea within a mile of the Dee, still opens on 11 February and closes at the end of September. The differences between these dates, and indeed 15 January

The author with a fish of over 50 lb. The scales weighed no more than 50lb. The fish was 52in in length and should, according to Sturdy, have weighed 60lb. It was tailed by the angler fly-fishing alone.

when a few rivers open, are not particularly important save that the earlier closing dates in the autumn undoubtedly save a number of fish and allow them up to the spawning beds. When we come to the Tweed and some of the smaller rivers in the south-west of England, where fishing is allowed into December while spawning is in full swing, then we reach a situation where the reason for any legislation at all seems to have no foundation.

Obviously the netting close season was established for the express purpose of allowing a sufficiency of salmon to have free access to the spawning beds. The dates most generally applicable, 26 August to 11 February, were reckoned to allow enough fish into the river both at the beginning and before the end of the close season to restock the whole river. It must be remembered that these laws were enacted when netting was carried out both by professional netsmen and riparian owners anywhere throughout the length of the river. In 'the bad old days', indeed in my lifetime, the Spey was netted beyond Craigellachie and the Dee as far up as Banchory. At the same time the law proscribed the killing of 'unclean' fish. This has always been interpreted as referring to kelts. But the kelt, the already spawned fish, is the only salmon which is of no possible value to the river. It is fully time that the term 'unclean' was interpreted to mean what I believe those who originally promulgated this law intended – that is salmon full of roe and not yet spawned.

Immediately we face a difficulty which would appear to have no obvious solution. In a sense every salmon entering the river is a spawning fish. Every fish has roe in it, partly or well developed. At what point, if we refer to the unspawned fish, can the salmon be described as 'clean' or 'unclean'? I opine that the reason that the present interpretation of the word 'unclean' refers specifically to spawned fish is that it has been impossible to define when an unspawned fish becomes 'unclean'. At what point in the development of its roe is it no longer a 'clean' salmon. It is perhaps relevant here to note that as late as Edwardian times the main spring fishing in the river Dee was all above Aboyne and right up to the Linn of Dee. The river was netted as far up as Banchory and fished by the rod above that. Today only the odd 'clean' salmon is caught above Aboyne in the early season and it is usually not until the second week in May that any stock of fish is seen above Ballater. There is no doubt at all in my mind that the 'clean' fish that then formed the early-spring fishing, in these upper beats were all kelts. That they were well mended kelts such as we used to catch in the Don in February and March, easily mistaken by the inexperienced for clean fish, was almost certainly due to the fact that almost the only salmon allowed to reach the spawning beds of the upper river, and not netted in the bottom fifteen miles, were those autumn fish which entered after the nets closed on 26 August. So the Thinking

*Iceland. The best and surest shot to hook a fish on the whole river –
running fish usually jump the falls and do not use the ladder.*

Fisherman about to enjoy his autumn holiday faces a dilemma. As a
sportsman he faces ethical problems at every turn. He does not, for instance,
care for hind stalking in late winter and would be horrified if he killed a beast
which still had a calf of the year following her. But he knows that the surplus
hinds have to be killed so must be prepared to overlook his inborn dislike of
killing possibly pregnant females at the only time that the law permits. He
would not dream of hunting a fox when the vixen might be carrying young
and disapproves of farmers shooting pigeons in springtime when they have
young in the nest and objects strongly to such bodies as the Forestry
Commission encouraging their foresters to kill roe deer, capercaillie and
even blackgame, at any time of year, because they damage the plantations.
He is unhappy shooting driven grouse in October if he is expected to kill one
or both of what is obviously a 'pair'. And he is always conscious stricken if he
shoots a goose and sees its mate circling around unwilling to leave its dying
lifelong companion. The same sort of problem faces the autumn salmon
fisherman. By late August the fish that have been in the river for some
weeks and often several months are beginning to look like a totally different
species to the lovely silvery blue and pink tinted creatures which entered in
the spring. By now the males have a thickened 'tartan' skin, a 'kype' growing

on their lower jaw and have lost the streamlined shape of the 'springer'. The females, also reddened overall, have a nasty grey look where their silver white bellies once showed and are already misshapen with enormous roes. These fish are now concerned only with preparing for spawning. Where salmon are still entering, fresh run, from the sea they too will be red in colour and full of roe. They will have a well-grown set of teeth and will head straight for the area of redds for which they are destined. With them, and easily distinguished by their appearance, may come a number of true 'spring' fish. These will have no developed roe, no teeth, and will be completely lacking in any redness. Whereas the former make hurriedly for the spawning beds the latter tend to hang about in the deeper pools of the lower river and will not run upstream until the new year.

It is, of course, an error to suppose that all salmon make upstream to the headwaters to spawn. Many fish spawn successfully if the water is unpolluted in the very lowest reaches of some of our rivers. The famous autumn run of Blue Cocks in the Spey never went as far as Craigellachie Bridge in any numbers and spawned mostly in the Gordon Castle water. Many of the autumn run fish in the Tweed spawn within ten miles of the sea. In practically every salmon river some fish spawn in little side streams quite close to the mouth. I have even seen salmon, a full dozen of them, actually spawning in a mill lade.

Having said that, there may be a certain distaste on the part of the fisherman in catching, and especially killing, these autumn salmon so near to their spawning time. I must point out that the only reason that the fish ever returns to the river at all is to spawn. Therefore every salmon returning from the sea is in a sense a spawning fish. Is it foolish to discriminate between one salmon and another on this score?

The fisherman must remember, too, that the salmon is now no longer a migratory fish and that, though still in its migratory travelling dress, it is in the process of assuming its natural river dress. It started in life as a fish which looked and behaved like a trout and is reverting to a trout-like fish in appearance. The only reason that these fish do not behave like very big cannibal trout in all respects is because their digestive systems are still atrophied and they cannot feed and, consequently, show little inclination to hunt. Were this not the case there would be no living thing, fish or insect, left in the river.

Nevertheless, just as we have postulated that the fasting fish never completely loses its habit of hunting and can therefore be caught by flies and baits, so it is with the autumn fish. But it is no longer a sea fish with a memory of hunting in the sea. It is now a river fish and will behave somewhat like a freshwater trout. You can catch large hand-reared trout

169

with anything you care to throw into the water, pellets, minnows, spoons or even flies. But you cannot catch the really big wild fish on flies. They are virtually all cannibals. If you want to catch one of these you must use a minnow or spoon. It is the same with these autumn salmon. They must be regarded as nothing other than big overgrown salmon parr and fished for as if they were overgrown trout.

The transition from summer fishing with the small fly into autumn fishing is gradual. The pace at which this takes place varies from season to season according to the weather and the temperature. From the end of August, in general, the salmon begin to disregard the small fly. Many fish will still be looking at the surface and will be interested in little lures. But increasingly, as every day passes, more and more fish cease to observe the surface and become interested in what is going on around themselves rather than what is above them. They are remembering their trout-like existence of their early years in the river. They are becoming giant salmon parr and will behave like giant trout. They will no longer be interested in flies and small creatures of the surface layers of the river. Like very big trout, these giant salmon parr become cannibals by nature. The Thinking Fisherman recognizes this fact and adjusts his techniques accordingly.

River Vididalsa, Iceland. Returning home at midnight in late June.

If the river remains at summer levels it is usually sufficient to continue to fish with the floating line used with the small fly but to put on a much larger and heavier fly. It does not really matter whether this is $1\frac{1}{2}$in, a 2in or even a 3in fly. On the whole the fish tend to take the larger sizes rather more freely than the smaller, but in lower water these big flies may spend much of their time catching rocks, weeds and other obstructions on the bottom. If the river rises then flies of at least $2\frac{1}{2}$in to 3in must be used and it is advantageous to change the floating line for a sunk line. The question of what type of fly to use at this time of year again poses itself. There is absolutely no doubt at all that the Waddington type is the most successful. But landing the maximum number of fish may not always be the ultimate aim of the fisherman. For instance, personally I prefer to use single-hooked flies, inefficient though they may be in hooking. As I do not intend to kill most of the fish I catch at this time of year I do not mind 'pulls' and lost fish. For those who wish to take home as many fish as possible treble hooks are the thing.

The Thinking Fisherman may well ask himself why it is that these now much larger flies are so much more successful than the small greased-line flies which he has been using throughout the summer. The month of September shows a bigger fall in temperature between the first and the thirtieth day than in any similar period of the year. At the end of August the river may well be running, on a hot afternoon, at over 60° F. By the end of September the temperature will have dropped to less than the magic 48° F even in mid-afternoon, and considerably lower in the now much longer night. Even if the salmon is still behaving and 'thinking' like a migrating sea fish imprinted with a behaviour pattern acquired in the sea, it would still be ignoring small surface baits. Its sea feeding at these temperature would be on fish and other creatures which lived well away from the surface. Its river feeding would also reflect this.

By September the salmon is probably no longer influenced by its sea life and habits. It has reverted to being a river fish. As we have already said it has become an overgrown parr and behaves like a very big trout. Its fully grown river teeth give it away. It is now a ferocious cannibal.

I would end this book with a plea to all my fellow fishermen. If you enjoy the sport of catching late autumn salmon that have been in the river for several months and are very near spawning do not, I beg you, kill more than you need for home consumption. Remember that these fish will beget the next generation. Kill them all and you have destroyed the river. Think, too, that the beautiful silver springer you have caught earlier in the year may well have been the offspring of a fish you caught and spared some four or five years earlier.

Appendix A

The best explanation of what the fish sees and cannot see was written in *Fly-fishing* by Dr J. C. Mottram at the beginning of the century and is reproduced below.

SOME OPTICAL PROBLEMS

The optics of angling are always of interest, so without excuse one can discuss one or two points that seem to me to require further elucidation. Suppose one were to stand on the bottom of a river and look upwards, what would be seen? First, the surface of the water would look like a vast mirror, reflecting everywhere the river-bed—everywhere except directly above, where would appear a hole in the mirror; through this hole a view is obtained of the world above the water. In the centre there will be seen a more or less circular patch of sky; and forming, as it were, a frame to it, would be seen the earth, distant hills, trees, bushes, river banks, etc, all much dwarfed as regards height. Outside this frame and sharply bounding the hole will be seen a dark iridescent ring; into this dark ring the bases of the hills, trees, and river banks gradually fade and are lost to view; in fact, this black ring obscures all things that are only a little above the surface of the water. It is because the light that comes from these low-lying things is almost entirely reflected at the surface of the water that this black ring occurs, for it is in this region, at the outer edge of the hole, that the rays of light, coming from low-lying objects, enter the water, and because very little of their light penetrates the water they are lost to view in darkness. For this reason objects very little above the surface of the water cannot be seen; objects a little higher are somewhat veiled in this darkness, and only objects that are considerably above the water level appear undimmed.

What the angler wishes to know is, at what angle is this veiling of objects sufficient to make for concealment? On this point I have made experimental observations. To my eyes the veiling appears to be sufficient at about 80° to the vertical. Perhaps, now that all are motorists, I can make my meaning

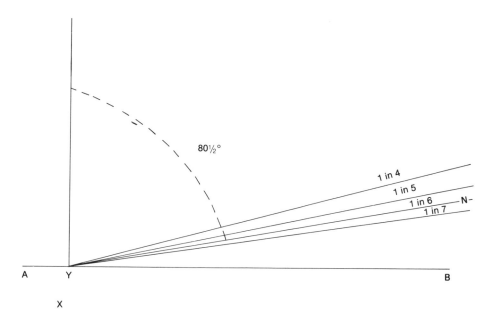

Fig 1

clearer by speaking in grades: AB=the surface of the water; X=a fish below it; Y=a point on the surface of the water above the fish; YN=a grade of 1 in 6, or $80\frac{1}{2}°$ to the vertical. All objects beneath YN appear to me to be sufficiently veiled; that is, an angler distant 30ft. from a fish is sufficiently veiled if he does not place any part of himself more than 5ft. above the water; also if he goes to within 15ft. of the fish, and does not show himself more than $2\frac{1}{2}$ft. above the water. This is how things appear to my eyes.

Photographs could, no doubt, be taken to show this veiling effect, but very long exposures would be required; short exposures would only give a silhouette of hills, trees, bushes, etc., against the sky; within them no detail would be visible, neither the veiling of their bases nor the dark ring without. Very long exposures would be very difficult to make, because the surface of the stillest water would not remain motionless for such a long period. However, these observations have been to some extent corroborated by experiments on fish at the riverside.

Walk up to a fish, making movements of the head, and notice when he first sees you, then make measurements of angles. I found that the fish seldom appear to see one until the grade reaches about 1 in 5—that is, when the angler's head is 5ft. above the water at a distance off of 25ft. 'But,' says the practical angler, 'I have seen fish scared at twenty yards away.' At once I ask, 'How were you holding your rod?' Of course, sometimes the angler will make such vivid contrasts with his background that the veiling will not be sufficient until grades of perhaps 1 in 7 or 1 in 8 have been reached, but this I find is uncommon. In the vast majority of cases I feel sure it is the rod and not the angler that scares the fish; the rod and the line too. I know of fish that fly for safety when they see the line extending towards them, and are gone before the fly reaches water. Highly varnished rods are a pleasure to handle, but will not a mat surface catch more fish?

For similar reasons it is better to be behind bushes and hedges; their tops are seldom so abrupt that one cannot find somewhere to peep through. Thus placed, it is possible to drop a fly on the water, round one side or over the top, without showing the rod top above the bush, whereas when in front of the bush the rod top must be raised above the bush to clear the back cast. The angler must remember to look to his rod more than to himself when stalking a fish.

In conclusion, one would say an angler who keeps himself and his rod below a grade of 1 in 6 is out of view. Possibly a grade of 1 in 5 is often sufficient, or even lesser grades, when the angler makes little contrast with his surroundings. On the other hand, grades of 1 in 7 or 1 in 8 may be necessary when the angler strongly contrasts with his surroundings.

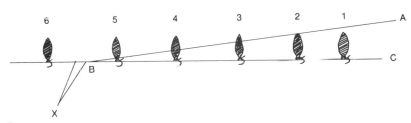

Fig 2

Diagram No. 2 shows why the fish first sees the wings of a fly floating towards it—namely, because it is the top of the wing that first appears above the grade AB (of 1 in 6 to 1 in 8). All things below AB are invisible to the fish because they are lost in darkness, or, to be more correct, in prismatic colours. ABC may be called the invisible angle, and in this the angler must keep.

Thus theory and practice agree. One can quite well understand the annoyance of an angler, who has practised his art for some decades, when he is told that, according to theory, he is not fishing correctly; one can understand his coming to regard theorists with a great hatred, his coming to the conclusion that much theory spoils sport. But in this case it is different.

175

He is pleased, perhaps gratified, by this confirmation of his practice. Therefore he becomes interested in the problem, and by the addition of interest his sport is more pleasant for him. To know is a pleasure, or should be; hence the striving for knowledge, even fishing knowledge, both theoretical and practical.

Appendix B

PHEROMONES AND MIGRATIONS

(A pheromone is a substance secreted and released by an animal for detection and response by another of the same species.)

The first proof that it was the 'odour' of the water that enables salmon to return to their own river and own branch stream was made in 1926. A Dr Crathie took 259 fish with cut olfactory nerves and 254 normal fish from a tributary and released them lower down the main river. The normal fish returned again to their own tributary, but those with cut olfactory nerves returned at random to any tributary stream or rivulet. Similar experiments conducted by Wisby and Hasler in 1954 and by Japanese scientists in 1967 confirmed the evidence of the significance of olfaction in the orientation and route determination of migrating salmon. These experiments strongly supported the theory that it is the 'mixture' of odours which is particular to each river, tributary and stream that allows the salmon to follow the correct route back to its own spawning area.

That the remembrance of the odours of the river water in the area in which it hatched might be 'imprinted' in its mind and allow the fish to find its way back seems to be perfectly feasible. But the idea that an 'imprinted' remembrance could enable a salmon smolt to find its way to its ocean feeding grounds, of which it has no previous knowledge or experience, is clearly unacceptable. Nevertheless it is, I believe, olfaction which directs the fish on its journey, monitors it on its proper route and brings it home again. Whereas it is the odour of the river water which may finally direct him home to his destined spawning bed it is a different odour which controls not only his outward passage as a smolt but most of his return in more than a thousand miles of unsignposted ocean.

This odour derives from the pheromones secreted and released by migrating salmon, both mature fish and smolts, on their outward journey and the return, and which forms a 'trail' which the smolts can follow as easily as a bloodhound can follow a man's footsteps several days old.

It is perhaps worth noting that when a dam which prevents fish running is built, trout and salmon collect in the pool immediately below vainly waiting for an opportunity to run upstream to spawn. But after a year or two, when there have been no fish spawning above and no more young fish descending, the trail of pheromones from the upper waters no longer exists. Now the pool becomes deserted – the trail is cold.

How strong is the 'scent' created by these pheromones? No one yet knows. It has been suggested that one atom in 500 million is sufficient. Other authorities hold that no more than one part in a million million suffices. With the miserable sense of smell that we humans possess compared with that of animals such figures are meaningless.

Appendix C

We have already indicated that the trout wet-fly does not usually represent a 'fly' but rather, either a nymph, or a fish. The salmon fly definitely does not represent an insect – it is too big – but almost certainly represents a fish. Let us look at it for a moment.

The salmon fly

At first glance there does not appear to be anything very fish-like about this object. Let us, however, remove the hook.

Salmon fly without hook

This still does not look much like a fish. So let us try again. Let us put this object made of feathers into the water and hold it steady against a current flowing past it.

The same in a current

By sketching in the missing portions we now have an object which gives a very fair representation of a fish. And when we remember that all salmon flies without exception have bright or partly bright bodies which represent the light underparts of a fish, we can see how our fly, with the hook acting as a keel and keeping it right way up, can deceive the salmon fairly successfully.

But the point that now arises is whether this simulation is achieved as successfully with the standard type of fly as it might be. I do not think that it is.

The first and most obvious weakness lies in the hook itself. To you and me this large appendage hanging down below the fly successfully destroys any illusion we may have about the fly looking like a small fish. Fortunately for us, however, the salmon is not cognizant of a fly as such, but he is familiar with small fish, and it would seem that he is, when fully aroused, prepared to overlook this quite unnatural extension and to 'see' only what he wants to see, i.e. the feathers and body which do somewhat resemble a fish. But it seems that there are limits to this credulity, this simplicity of mind and purpose. In heavy coloured water the hook is not so obvious as to deter the fish from his purpose. But in a low, clear river it is sometimes found that the fish is not so eager to take. Custom has ordained that under these circumstances a smaller fly shall be used, and whereas, as everyone who has fished any of our northern rivers in mid-March or early April will agree, the salmon does not take them nearly so avidly as he does the bigger fly in February, they do offer a certain measure of success.

Now, as I have said, in my view it is absolutely wrong to change down in size of fly; and I have found by experience that more success is achieved by sticking to the right size of fly even in dead low and clear water, than by using anything smaller. But, likewise, I have found that a much lighter type of standard hook is successful under these circumstances where the ordinary heavy early spring hook may fail. For many years I was under the impression that this was because it allowed the fly to swim higher in the water. I now believe that, whereas a failure to fish deep with the sunk fly is at any time to detract from one's chance, my lighter hooks had a much smaller gape and that what I lost by fishing too shallow was more than compensated for by the fact that my hook was far less obvious.

I can only reaffirm my belief that the standard types of hook used for spring salmon flies suffer from many disadvantages which should not be encountered. They are archaic in design for the purpose for which they are required.

Consider also the matter of the 'set' of the fly in the water. The fly is attached to and supported by the gut which is of considerably lower specific gravity than the steel of the hook. It follows, therefore, that the hook, especially since the bulk of its weight is 'aft', must lie in the water at a distinct angle to the horizontal and, depending upon the strength of the current, must move through the water more or less at this angle. What about our nice fish-like illusion now?

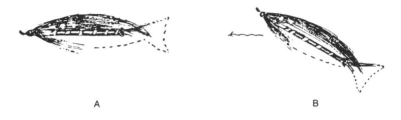

A   B

'Set' of fly in water

A is not too bad at all. But unfortunately B is really what happens. And fly-tiers have long realized, if not that this is actually what happens, at least that certain modifications have to be made in the tying of the fly if it is to be a success.

For instance, look at any big fly on a heavy hook.

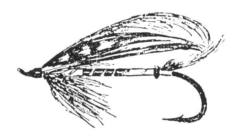

Fly on heavy hook

You will note that the wing is set at an angle to the body of the fly and that the hackle is not very long and invariably of some bright-coloured feathers. The reason is that compensation must be made for this angle at which the fly will swim.

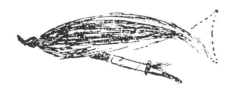

The same in water

181

The wing is set at such an angle to the body that it (the wing) will be horizontal in the water. The short hackle on the neck of the fly compensates for the upward lift of the front of the body, the bright upturned tail for the droop at the back of the body. Further, in many flies the body is tied in different colours and tones. Almost without exception, the forward portions of these bodies are solid and bright (i.e. black dubbing with tinsel as in Jock Scott, Mar Lodge, Ackroyd) and less solid (some colour such as yellow) behind. This is pure camouflage and has the effect of breaking up the very unnatural line of the body which lies at an impossible angle for the illusion.

I cannot be satisfied that in this age of reason and progress we have to accept such an obvious makeshift merely because it has been handed down to us from the 'dark ages'. The one point which seems never to have been realized by the makers of fishing tackle is that when you alter the scale of an article you must basically alter its design also. A rowing boat built to scale the size of the *Queen Mary* would break up at once and the *Queen Mary* scaled down to the size of a rowing boat would probably sink. An angel of the same weight and stature as a man would require, as Professor Haldane has pointed out, a chest 4ft in depth to hold the muscles necessary for flight. A mouse the size of an elephant could not stand up without breaking its legs – and so it goes on. When you alter the scale you must alter the design if the article is to 'work'. (For those interested in the technicalities this is because in size we are dealing generally with two distinct properties, the area and the mass. The area varies as the square of the linear dimensions, the mass as the cube. If you double the length, roughly speaking you quadruple the area, but you increase the mass eight times.)

The design of a fly is excellent in trout sizes. Here the small weight of the hook acting on a short lever (the shank) is of little effect in tipping the fly off its correct axis. But when we come to salmon sizes the story is quite different. An overgrown trout fly now has relatively much less surface to buoy it up, and the hook is of far greater mass and acts at the end of a much longer lever. It is little short of a miracle that such a lure can catch a fish in any but streams so fast that these flies are forced to lie horizontally. Here, I believe, is the main reason why salmon are so difficult to catch on a fly in still, deep pools, but can easily be caught on a bait.

The answer to this problem seems to me to be simple. If you accept the fact that your fly looks like a fish to the salmon, then you must redesign your shank and hook so that it swims like a fish, i.e. horizontally in the water.

If you are wedded to the conception of a fly which swims upright and which is 'fishy-looking' only when seen from the side, then you must (a) reduce the size of the hook and (b) see that its weight is counter-balanced by a like amount of weight in the head. It requires neither extraordinary imagination nor yet much ingenuity to suggest several different ways of doing this. My illustration shows two of many possibilities.

Flies 'swimming' horizontally

But, again, when we look at the typical salmon fly either from above, underneath or end on, it loses its resemblance to a fish because it is far too thin. It looks something like this:

Flies 'swimming' horizontally

A spinning bait, however, which many believe catches salmon more effectively than a fly, looks like a fish in shape from whatever angle you look at it. Is there any sense, then, in fishing with a fly which only looks like what it is meant to represent when seen from one point of view? Patently not!

In examining the fly there are other considerations besides those of its efficiency as a 'lure' which require analysis. Is the large salmon fly an efficient article for hooking and landing fish?

Here, I think, there can be no two opinions. It is not an efficiently designed article. The original 'fish-hook' from which the pattern of salmon-fly hook has evolved almost without modification was constructed in such a way that (1) it was simple to make; (2) was efficient for holding a bait and hooking the fish which tried to eat that bait. Invariably the bait covered the point and the barb, and the hook was made on the assumption that the fish actually tried to mouth and swallow the bait it carried.

The salmon-fly hook, however, does none of these things. It carries no bait on its gape or point; this is all carried on the shank. The salmon does not attempt to mouth and swallow it, or even to pass it through the gills as it does a worm. The fish merely takes the fly in its mouth, turns away with it (sometimes!) and, as soon as it becomes aware that it is not a juicy little fish, attempts to get rid of it. A coarse fish angler who threaded his worm on to the shank, or placed his paste pellet there and left the whole of the gape and point of the hook uncovered would be somewhat astonished if he ever succeeded in hooking a fish. The salmon fisherman who does almost the same thing is surprised when he does not!

Consider how the salmon takes one of these big flies. Only in exceptional cases does he grip it from behind. The normal method is to take it while the fly is swimming sideways with its axis more or less at right angles to that of the fish. Now a 3in fly has a gape of about 1in, and we must suppose that if the salmon looks on the fly as a small fish he must entirely disregard the hook which trails down below it. We must also suppose that in going for it, the salmon aims to get the feathered body of the fly in the centre of his opened mouth. If we regard this body as being $\frac{1}{2}$in in depth when in the water and all lying on top of the gape of the hook, the fish must open its mouth at the very least $2\frac{1}{2}$in if it is going to clear the gape of the hook by the merest fraction. We can safely say that to be sure of clearing it, the width of the opened mouth must be 3in. Next time you catch a 7lb salmon open its mouth 3in and see what it looks like! It is quite obvious that no salmon attempts to do such a thing. It follows therefore that in taking the fly either the fish misses the gape altogether by going too far forward to get it into its mouth at all, in which case when the fish lets go, the hook merely slides round the lower jaw and turns it outwards in the mouth; or else it hits the gape with its lower jaw and turns it outwards in the mouth. When now it lets go, the hook's point will penetrate something in all probability, but its chances of driving in much more than skin deep seem to be rather less than 50 per cent.

Leaving aside all theory and conjecture and writing from the practical experience of many years of fly-fishing, I have no doubt whatever that with all its shortcomings, the standard fly, properly fished, is more efficient judged as a lure than any bait; but it is grossly inefficient mechanically when it comes to hooking and playing a fish. I know that in our northern rivers I have caught as many, if not rather more, fish on the fly in the early spring than others fishing the bait on the same beat. But I also know that for every fish I have caught I have lost (this includes 'pulls' and 'touches') at least two fish with these standard flies: and any honest fly-fisherman will confess to at least this proportion of losses. The bait fisherman, by comparison, tempts far fewer fish to his lure (because, I think, it is a poorer representation in action than a fly), but he lands a far greater proportion of those fish which do attempt to take. And the reason is that the design of his tackle is infinitely superior when it comes to hooking.

As a result of these observations I have been driven to start from the beginning and to design an entirely new type of salmon fly which must, I am sure, be a better lure in so far as it swims at the proper angle in the water, appears the right shape from whatever angle is viewed and retains the advantage of light and life given to the standard fly by its feather construction. And it will also be a better mechanical device for hooking and playing a fish which has been tempted to take.

Round, or keel-less, fly

This fly is round, i.e. has no keel and can swim in any position and is still 'upright'. When in the water the long hackle feathers adopt a natural 'streamline' and the whole bait assumes the shape of a fish from whatever angle it is looked at.

The special features otherwise are:

A. In order to ensure that the fly shall swim in a horizontal position even in slack currents the forward end of the shank is made somewhat heavier than the after end. It will be realized, however, that under normal circumstances this refinement is not altogether necessary. The triangle attached to the after end of the shank offers relatively much greater surface for its weight than does the bend and point in a normal 8/0 hook. This has an effect of overcoming the tendency in the tail of the fly to sink.

B. The hackles are long enough to stream back as far as the hook link. This gives the body of the fly a torpedo or fish-like shape. The treble-hooks form the tail.

C. The body is constructed on similar lines to any other salmon fly body. It is not, however, necessary to camouflage this by breaking up its line, though to do so will do no harm if the taste of the fisherman using it calls for it.

D. The hooks are linked to the shank. The object of this is purely mechanical. The leverage on the hook of a 3in solid fly is very severe. To lessen this leverage it is only common sense to shorten the length of the lever. This I have done by linking the triangle to the shank. The triangle is kept from falling out of line with the shank by a stiff nylon bristle attached to both.

E. The hooks are made by a standard treble with as short a shank as possible. The size of treble in an 8/0 fly is 6/0, and in a 6/0 fly is a 4/0 treble.

Theory is all very well, but how does this fly work in practice?

The earliest prototypes were tied most indifferently by myself some years ago. They proved extraordinarily successful. The very first I tried down the Rock Pool at Phonas in the Spey and the first fish that took it (incidentally it was the first of the season from either bank on that beat) came so gently that I was only aware of 'something' having stopped the fly. Yet this 16-pounder was perfectly hooked in the lower jaw with two of the points of the treble deeply embedded. With this fly I touched four fish and landed them all. With my second fly the tale was exactly the same. I never pulled a fish but I landed it.

That season failed to give more than an indication of the possibilities of this type of fly. I found it quite impossible to get a manufacturer to make forged linked shanks for me, and my prototypes were made with gut loops and eyes. These did not stand up to the wear and tear of playing fish and all broke eventually.

Confirmation of my own early impressions came in a letter from an angler with whom I was then unacquainted. He wrote from the Shin: 'One of our party . . . decided to try out your fly. I did not try them until the second week, when, in an effort to improve our bag, which up to then had been very small, we gave his ghillie the silver-grey 'fly' and told him to try it out one evening. That evening the ghillie brought in two fish and reported the loss (by breaking) of a third. We immediately telephoned Edinburgh and asked for a dozen flies to be sent by return, and when they came we caught several more fish with them.' This particular lot of flies was made with gut loops joining on the triangle end, and as the writer observed, this was a point of weakness. It was sufficiently striking as an experiment, however, for another of the same party to write and tell me that so highly thought of were these flies by the local ghillies and fishermen that when they left 'we could have sold our remaining stock of your flies for £5 apiece easily'.

The following year, however, I had the first properly-constructed flies made – and I have fished with them now for several seasons.

The results have surprised me. In 1950, for example, we started fishing the Inverness-shire Garry, which is the fly river *par excellence* in my view, with ordinary standard pattern 8/0 flies. I kept a careful record of the number of fish hooked or pulled and the numbers caught. Until the end of March the figures were 47 fish caught with fly, 96 lost on fly and a further 34 pulled on fly. At the end of March I received from Messrs. Alexander Martin (Glasgow), whom I had persuaded to manufacture them, the first batch of properly-constructed 'Waddington' flies of 8/0 size. We used these throughout April and early May under the worst fishing conditions – very few fish, very big water, very cold weather – that I ever remember at this time of year. The result was: 'Waddington' flies, 55 fish killed, 4 lost (broken), 1 lost (came off hooks), 3 pulls; standard flies, 13 fish killed, 27 lost and pulled. I think these results speak for themselves and need no comment beyond the statement that the Garry river is one of the fastest streams in Scotland and the fish average 18lb in weight. I also tried these flies on the Gordon Castle water of the Spey.

I do not want to bore the reader with unnecessary detail and will content myself with saying that the success of these flies was so striking that after the first day's use the ghillies, some of whom had been over forty years on the water, opined that the standard fly was virtually eclipsed. From so conservative a source as the older generation of Spey ghillies this is praise indeed.

I have no hesitation now after considerable experience in their use in stating that for spring fishing these flies are so superior to the standard type of fly that I find it difficult to believe that anyone who has ever given them a fair trial would willingly revert to the old 'normal' types. Personally, the idea of losing a fish, which after all nowadays is worth anything from between £5 and £10 as a saleable article of food, through using inefficient tackle of any sort seems not only silly but verging on lunacy!

With the small greased-line sizes I was at first disappointed. The original samples made by Alexander Martin neither looked right to me, nor did they appear to be such good lures from the point of view of getting fish to take them as the normal types of flies. That they were infinitely surer once the fish had taken was unquestionable, but this did not compensate for the fact that I had formed the impression that they were not so readily taken in summer heights of water as flies on ordinary low-water hooks.

Now, however, I have discovered what was wrong. The dressing was too bunchy and the triangles too big. I was, at first, doubtful of the wisdom of using very small triangles of size 16 and 18. But trial has satisfied me that they are probably even more efficient than the larger sizes. It is not uncommon to find all three hooks embedded out of sight in the fish's jaws or mouth after landing him. With a flatter, less ample dressing and armed with much smaller triangles the greased-line low-water sizes of this fly now bear, in my view, the same relationship to the single and double standard flies to these sizes as do the 8/0 'Waddington' flies to the normal single-hooked flies of this size for sunk-line fishing. I would now use no other. Alas, I have no financial interest in the sale of these flies!

(Reproduced from Richard Waddington's book, *Salmon Fishing*, Faber and Faber Ltd, 1959.)

Index

(Italic numerals denote page numbers of illustrations.)